Gender Mainstreaming in Information and Communications

A Reference Manual for Governments and Other Stakeholders

Joan Ross Frankson

Commonwealth Secretariat

Gender Management System Series

Gender Management System Handbook

Using Gender-Sensitive Indicators: A Reference Manual for Governments and Other Stakeholders

Gender Mainstreaming in Development Planning: A Reference Manual for Governments and Other Stakeholders

Gender Mainstreaming in Finance: A Reference Manual for Governments and Other Stakeholders

Gender Mainstreaming in the Public Service: A Reference Manual for Governments and Other Stakeholders

Gender Mainstreaming in Education: A Reference Manual for Governments and Other Stakeholders

Gender Mainstreaming in Trade and Industry: A Reference Manual for Governments and Other Stakeholders

Gender Mainstreaming in Agriculture and Rural Development: A Reference Manual for Governments and Other Stakeholders

Gender Mainstreaming in Information and Communications: A Reference Manual for Governments and Other Stakeholders

Gender and Equal Employment Opportunities: A Reference Manual for Governments and Other Stakeholders

A Quick Guide to the Gender Management System

A Quick Guide to Using Gender-Sensitive Indicators

A Quick Guide to Gender Mainstreaming in Development Planning

A Quick Guide to Gender Mainstreaming in Finance

A Quick Guide to Gender Mainstreaming in the Public Service

A Quick Guide to Gender Mainstreaming in Education

A Quick Guide to Gender Mainstreaming in Trade and Industry

A Quick Guide to Gender Mainstreaming in Agriculture and Rural Development

A Quick Guide to Gender Mainstreaming in Information and Communications

A Quick Guide to Gender and Equal Employment Opportunities

Commonwealth Secretariat
Marlborough House
Pall Mall, London SW1Y 5HX
United Kingdom

© Commonwealth Secretariat, May 2000

Designed and published by the Commonwealth Secretariat. Printed in the United Kingdom by Abacus Direct. Wherever possible, the Commonwealth Secretariat uses paper sourced from sustainable forests or from sources that minimise a destructive impact on the environment.

Copies of this publication can be ordered from:
The Publications Manager, Information and Public Affairs Division, Commonwealth Secretariat, Marlborough House, London SW1Y 5HX, UK.
Tel: +44 (0)20 7747 6342;
Fax: +44 (0)20 7839 9081;
E-mail:
r.jones-parry@commonwealth.int

Price: £8.99
ISBN: 0-85092-602-5

Web sites:
http://www.thecommonwealth.org/gender
http://www.thecommonwealth.org
http://www.youngcommonwealth.org

Contents

Preface

In 1996, Commonwealth Ministers Responsible for Women's Affairs mandated the Commonwealth Secretariat to develop the concept of the Gender Management System (GMS), a comprehensive network of structures, mechanisms and processes for bringing a gender perspective to bear in the mainstream of all government policies, programmes and projects. The success of the GMS depends upon a broad-based partnership in society in which government consults and acts co-operatively with the other key stakeholders, who include civil society and the private sector. The establishment and strengthening of gender management systems and of national women's machineries was the first of 15 government action points identified in the 1995 Commonwealth Plan of Action on Gender and Development.

This reference manual has been produced to assist member governments in meeting their commitment to implementing the Plan of Action. It is hoped that it will be used by public service commissioners, policy-makers, planners and others, in conjunction with other publications relating to the particular national context.

The manual is intended to serve for accessible reference to aid users in using a GMS to mainstream gender in the public service ministry of national governments. It is part of the Gender Management System Series, which provides tools and sector-specific guidelines for gender mainstreaming. This manual is intended to be used in combination with the other documents in the series, particularly the *Gender Management System Handbook*, which presents the conceptual and methodological framework of the GMS. This manual is also available in an abridged form under the title *A Quick Guide to Gender Mainstreaming in Information and Communications*.

The development of the GMS Series has been a collaborative effort between the Commonwealth Secretariat's Gender and Youth Affairs Division and many individuals and groups. Their contributions to the thinking behind the GMS are gratefully acknowledged. In particular, I would like to thank the following: all those member governments who supported the development of the GMS and encouraged us to move the project forward; participants at the first GMS meeting in Britain in February 1997 and at the GMS Workshop in Malta in April 1998, who provided invaluable conceptual input and feedback; and the Steering Committee on the Plan of Action (SCOPA). I am also most grateful to: Joan Ross Frankson, who wrote the text of this manual; Daniel Woolford, Consultant Editor of the GMS publications, who edited it; and the staff of the Gender Affairs Department, Gender and Youth Affairs Division, Commonwealth Secretariat, particularly Ms Eleni Stamiris, former Director of the Division, who took the lead in formulating the GMS concept and mobilising the various stakeholders in its development and Dr Rawwida Baksh-Soodeen, Project Co-ordinator of the GMS Series, who guided the project through to publication.

We hope that this resource series will be of genuine use to you in your efforts to mainstream gender.

Nancy Spence
Director
Gender and Youth Affairs Division
Commonwealth Secretariat

Executive Summary

This reference manual provides guidelines for mainstreaming gender into the functions of Ministries of Information and Communication. Its main objective is to assist governments in advancing gender equality in their countries, especially through the establishment and operation of a Gender Management System as a means of mainstreaming gender across all government policies, plans, programmes and projects. It presents an extensive list of recommendations for action, grouped under a series of strategic objectives. It includes a questionnaire for conducting a gender impact analysis as well as various tools designed to assist ministry personnel in putting gender on the agenda of their activities: conducting gender impact analysis, collecting data on problems faced by women and men in the sector, using gender-sensitive language, and creating linkages with women's media networks at regional and global levels.

While this manual is aimed primarily at governments, it may also be of use to private-sector and civil society organisations that wish to advance gender equality and equity in the sector. It is designed to present a menu of options and action points that users may adapt to specific national contexts.

A Gender Framework for the Information Sector

Gender is a concept that refers to a system of roles and relationships between women and men that are determined by the political, economic, social and cultural context rather than by biology. One's biological sex is a natural given; gender, on the other hand, is socially constructed. We are taught 'appropriate' behaviour and attitudes, roles and activities, expectations and desires. It is this learned behaviour that makes up women's and men's gender identity and determines their gender roles.

In some regions of the Commonwealth, recent gender analysis reveals the emergence of male disadvantage in certain areas, especially young men (for example in educational attainment and access to health care). Where this occurs, a gendered approach can ensure that interventions address these inequalities appropriately. In most parts of the world, however, it is women who are disadvantaged. Therefore, since this manual is intended to advance gender equality and equity, much of its analysis focuses specifically on ways to improve women's standing in the information sector.

How are gender roles manifested in the social construct and what are the implications for women and men? Four areas are addressed: work, global resources and benefits, human rights and religion. In all these areas, women are disadvantaged in various ways in many countries of the world.

Objectivity is often held up as the main principle of journalism. But how does the assumption of objectivity find expression by individual communicators socialised into accepting unequal relationships between men and women as the norm? Once this reality is clear, the importance of raising gender awareness among writers, reporters, editors and all those involved in the creative process, becomes self-evident. The critical areas to target are: language, stereotyping and story selection.

Communicating gender equality requires journalists and other media practitioners to observe the ways that people may be marginalised because of their gender as well as race/ethnicity, class/caste, age and other such factors. Who gets coverage? From what perspective? Through which lens? Reflecting which stereotypes about people from different gender, race/ethnic, class and other groups? Are stories helping to advance gender equality and equity in society or are they angled in a way that upholds traditional attitudes and values?

Gender on the Global Agenda

Women and the media is a critical area of concern in the Platform for Action, signed by governments at the United Nations Fourth World Conference on Women in Beijing in 1995. The current development discourse on gender and media began in the 1970s within the framework of three international events and processes: the United Nations Decade for Women (1976-1985), the New International Information and Communication Order (NIICO) spearheaded by UNESCO, and the networking activities of women's movements worldwide.

The 1995 Commonwealth Plan of Action on Gender and Development includes 15 action points that are recommended for governments to take in order to advance gender equality and equity. These action points include: undertaking an advocacy role in partnership with the media, and using gender-sensitive and gender-inclusive language:

A consultative approach is required in mapping out actions to be taken by all the stakeholders. Such an approach, particularly with respect to the sensitive area of media content, fosters the development of democratic practices and offers broader possibilities for freedom of expression in civil society.

Gender Mainstreaming

Gender mainstreaming means integrating a gender equality perspective into all the mainstream activities of government, at the policy, programme and project levels. It involves:
+ forging and strengthening the political will to achieve gender equality and equity, at the local, national, regional and global levels;
+ incorporating a gender perspective into planning processes;
+ integrating a gender perspective into sectoral planning cycles;
+ using sex-disaggregated data in statistical analysis;
+ increasing the numbers of women in decision-making positions;
+ providing tools and training in gender analysis and gender planning to key personnel; and
+ forging linkages between governments, the private sector, civil society and other stakeholders to ensure a co-ordination of efforts and resources.

The strategy of mainstreaming has evolved out of efforts by the international women's movement to change the attitudes, assumptions, working practices and activities of public institutions which reproduce and contribute to gender inequalities.

Three possible approaches to policy are identified: gender-neutral policies are seen as having no significant gender dimension; gender-specific policies take into account gender differentials, and target women or men specifically, but leave the current distribution of resources and responsibilities intact; and gender-aware/redistributive/transformative policies seek to transform existing gender relations by changing the distribution of resources and responsibilities to make it more equitable.

The basic choice presented is whether media policy reflects, perpetuates, or challenges gender hierarchies. The latter approach involves the implementation of gender-aware/transformative policies and implies a proactive effort to: avoid stereotyping; ensure the equal participation of women and men in decision-making, agenda-setting and content-determining activities; and advance gender equality on all fronts.

The government ministry responsible for the information and (tele)communications sector is assumed to have the following functions in relation to the media: policy analysis and development; policy-making at the political/ministerial level; administration and implementation of policy (policy deployment); regulation; and government information and media services.

The depth of gender stereotyping among all those involved in the information and communications process needs to be both openly acknowledged and acted upon – training, guidelines and processes need to be established to counteract and break down established attitudes. The task requires political will and the allocation of additional human and financial resources. Benchmarks should be established and concrete work plans drawn up in respect to actions, mechanisms and processes throughout the system. A credible monitoring mechanism should be in place, as should standards of accountability. An understanding of the concept of gender should not be assumed. Steps should be taken to raise awareness among all levels of staff including the introduction of non-sexist language guidelines and gender-aware editorial practices.

The Gender Management System

The GMS is an approach to gender mainstreaming developed by the Commonwealth. The Gender Management System (GMS) is an integrated network of structures, mechanisms and processes designed to make governments more gender-aware; increase the numbers of women in decision-making positions within and outside government; facilitate the formulation of gender-sensitive policies, plans and programmes; and promote the advancement of gender equality and equity in society.

Gender and the Media

Today's media can deliver messages and symbols – imported or domestic – directly into almost every home. Unfortunately, however, they continue to perpetuate and reinforce negative, stereotypical images of both women and men, according to which the resort to violence on the part of some males is presented as a 'natural' and acceptable way of resolving conflicts, and which do not provide an accurate or realistic picture of women's multiple roles and contributions to an ever-changing world.

The mass media are major socialising agents in modern society. Where media systems are highly developed, people spend at least four hours a day watching television, listening to radio, and reading magazines and newspapers. Although in domestic viewing and listening situations, the decisions of the adult male in the household tend to prevail (Mytton, 1993; Lull, 1988), women are enthusiastic media users. The pattern of preferences is similar worldwide: men prefer sports, action-oriented programmes and information (especially news); women prefer popular drama, music, dance and other entertainment programmes (Sepstrup and Goonasekara, 1994; Bonder and Zurutuza, 1994). This is not to suggest that all men or women prefer these catagories of programmes, simply that this is the dominant trend observed by the researchers.

Gender differences are linked to power and influence in the mainstream media. Over 400 women communicators from 80 countries called the media "a male-dominated tool used by those in power," (Bangkok Declaration, 1994). According to the 1995 Global Media Monitoring Project, "it is evident that gender differences are linked to power and influence," and "news gathering and news reporting are rooted in a value system which accords higher status to men and 'the masculine'." The way the world is portrayed on television "serves to maintain entrenched power imbalances," and "this fits into a long history of the use of public displays of violence to maintain rankings of domination ..." (Eisler, 1996). News, for example, is more often being presented *by* women but it is still very rarely *about* women. According to the 1995 Global Media Monitoring Project, women comprised 43 per cent of journalists but only 17 per cent of those interviewed as experts or opinion makers.

Studies suggest that the presence of more women journalists and female experts voicing opinions in the media would create "significant role models for other women, stimulate female interest in public issues, and – perhaps – sometimes speak in the interests of and for women" (Sreberny-Mohammadi, 1994). Another solution is for the media to shift attention away from the traditional 'power' perspectives with respect to the top echelons of politics, government and business, and focus more on aspects that are more inclusive of women. This is not to suggest an abandonment of power and influence, but rather that the media broaden their horizons and seek greater inclusiveness and diversity in their reporting.

Most regions have seen a steady growth in the numbers, range and scope of women working in mainstream media, but women are much more likely to be concentrated in administrative than in the other occupational categories (i.e., production/editorial, design, and technical). Of all the women working in media, some 50 per cent are located in administration in contrast to five per cent on average in the technical field (Gallagher and von Euler, 1995). Women still lack the power to develop media policy, or to determine the nature and shape of media content. This is so even in North America, where a dramatic increase has been noted in women-owned media and in women's organisations working on media representation issues. Women's average share of posts at the top three levels of management is below 20 per cent in all media and all regions except for broadcasting in Latin America. Women are also a minority in the committees and boards that define and shape policy, holding just 12 per cent of these positions in broadcasting, and 9 per cent in the press.

Despite the general upward trend in their numbers and visibility women also drop out at a greater rate than men. The most commonly reported obstacle to career development reported by women is that of male attitudes. Women are constantly judged by male standards and performance criteria of what constitutes news and who constitutes a newsmaker, a gender bias which leads to discrimination in the awarding of assignments: many women journalists report being denied approval to cover beats such as science and technology, politics and economics. Women are also confronted by social disapproval since the critical, independent, assertive and self-assured approach required of journalists often runs counter to cultural norms for women.

It is widely accepted that greater involvement by women in both the technical and decision-making areas of communication and media would improve both the content of media coverage and the context in which women journalists work.

Gender-based stereotyping can be found in public and private, local, national and international media organisations – electronic, print, visual and audio. The media is often criticised for perpetuating images that reduce women to sex objects, and for promoting violence against women as 'entertainment'. Degrading images negatively affect women and distort men's attitudes towards women and children by fixing them to their physical attributes and making no recognition of the complex realities of their lives. Advertising, in particular, often offers lurid sexual innuendoes aimed at men and which demean women as appendages or reinforce the notion of women as mere objects.

In many developing countries, television fare is restricted by budget constraints. Imported programming, often old series in which the way women are portrayed may be outdated even in the country of origin, may dominate peak viewing times. While local programming is often expensive to produce and may lack sophistication, joint productions with local private companies, sensitive pre-screening of programmes from the developed countries and exchanges with other developing countries are some ways to improve this situation. National broadcasting entities can also foster partnerships with community groups using video for community development.

Gender stereotyping by the media leads women, men and children to develop false and stultifying views and expectations of themselves and others, and masks reality. When women and men fail to match up to the fantasy ideal created by the media, serious problems may arise. Both women and men may develop low self-esteem. Women are more likely to become depressed and accepting of abuse, while men are more likely to become frustrated and angry, leading to violent and abusive behaviour.

The high incidence of media violence worldwide – whether verbal, physical, psychological and/or sexual – is of great concern and has generated debate and research into just how media violence affects viewers, in particular children. Media violence is insidious since the viewer may perceive no visible long-term effects. It is appealing since it is so often linked with power, and it is shown as a quick way of resolving conflicts.

A 1995 study of US television programming concluded that "violence remains a pervasive, major feature of contemporary television programming, and it is coming from more sources and in greater volume than ever before." The study cited 1,846 individual acts of violence – ranging from violence that resulted in one or more fatalities, to threatening behaviour with a weapon. Media watchdog groups in all continents have proved most effective in raising public awareness of these issues.

The creation of alternative presses has opened new publishing opportunities for women. Worldwide networks of independent video makers and filmmakers are developing a variety of visual alternatives and narratives (Riano, 1994). Women are now able to move information around the globe even faster than some governments through watchdog networks that combine fax-trees, e-mail, postal services and word of mouth. The Beijing Platform for Action, in recognition of the important role of women's alternative media networks, calls for governments "to support the development of and finance, as appropriate, alternative media and the use of all means of communication to disseminate information to and about women and their concerns" (Paragraph 245e).

Ministries of Information and Communication can link up, support, and benefit from women's alternative media organisations in respect of their outreach, innovative uses of local culture, and their perspectives. A first step is to recognise their work, contribution and expertise by including their representatives in policy-making – on advisory boards, and editorial groups – and as experts in programming. Ministries may also seek to partner with women's alternative media networks for education purposes: in awareness-building workshops for ministry and public service broadcasting personnel, for public sensitisation campaigns, and for media awareness training in schools.

Women are making great strides in adopting electronic communications, and have benefited from the support and facilitation provided by proactive initiatives. Increased communication and sharing of knowledge among women, particularly in the South but also in Eastern Europe and remote communities in the North, has broadened the scope of on-line participation creating a more equitable global women's forum on-line. For many more women, using e-mail has become a routine part of their day-to-day lives.

The challenges and pitfalls of electronic communications include limited accessibility, information overload, language constraints, skill deficiencies, and lack of gender-sensitive training. Women in the developing South face particular challenges: limitations of e-mail only accounts (not having access to remote databases or Internet tools); limited infrastructure (difficulty in getting a phone line); and the high costs of data transmission (networks in the South often charge their users for all messages, both sent and received).

Existing literature on women's portrayal by, access to, and employment in the media is still heavily dominated by research from North America and Western Europe. Studies from other parts of the world, where they do exist, are often limited in their scope. Apart from the need to develop and strengthen databases about women and media, research should be used as the basis for action that productively enhances women's relationship to the media. The research should also be used to develop appropriate support materials.

In all regions the number of women in higher education journalism courses has been increasing. At the same time, few courses are tailored specifically for gender concerns even where courses in development communications exist. Women-specific training that is free is recommended particularly in the area of electronic communications. Studies have recorded different tendencies between women and men in their ease and use of electronic communications; for example, men start with hands-on exploration, while women first want to know how it all works. Women have less access to electronic communications and less ownership of equipment. They are therefore not so proactive in learning the new technologies and need more initial encouragement and training.

Strategies and Recommendations for Action

Governments may wish to adapt these recommendations to suit their particular national circumstances and priorities. In addition, some specific tools are provided in this manual for use in carrying out the recommended actions. Since in most countries the media are overwhelmingly male-controlled and portray women largely in terms of limited stereotypes, the strategies recommended here focus mainly on closing the gender gap for women. In countries where male marginalisation is an emerging problem, attention should be paid to the role of the media in reversing this trend. There is also a need to focus on the role of the media in re-socialising both women and men, and changing traditional attitudes, behaviours and roles that perpetuate gender stereotypes and inequalities.

The policy environment

✦ Review existing policies with a view to integrating a gender perspective aimed at enhancing women's skills, knowledge, access, and participation in all types of media.
✦ Encourage the creation and/or strengthening of guidelines, codes of conduct or other self regulatory mechanisms for the media to eliminate gender-biased programming.

✦ Ensure gender balance in all government, parliamentary, state or public entities that consider media, advertising and telecommunications policy.
✦ Enact appropriate legislation against pornography and the projection of violence against women and children in the media.
✦ Abolish laws which effectively curb freedom of expression and/or freedom of association, and that result in discrimination against women.

Image and portrayal of women and men

✦ Promote balanced and diverse media portrayals of women as persons who bring to their positions many different life experiences to provide role models for young women.
✦ Provide positive role-models for young males and avoid reinforcing stereotypical images of masculinity and femininity that perpetuate gender inequalities.
✦ Promote the use of non-sexist, gender-sensitive language.
✦ Exclude stereotyped images, and violent and/or pornographic materials that discriminate against or that violate women's and children's rights.
✦ Increase the number of programmes for, by and about women.
✦ Increase women's participation, particularly in the portrayal of traditionally male-dominated areas of society linked to power and influence.
✦ Broaden sources – women, youth, indigenous people can speak on any issue and on all aspects of life.
✦ Create and strengthen media monitoring entities and encourage adequate consideration of consumer complaints against media content that portray women or men in a discriminatory way.

Employment

✦ Ensure equal employment opportunities for women at all levels of the media industry.
✦ Adopt positive action programmes so that women can reach their full potential as media professionals.
✦ Create opportunities to increase women's ownership of media houses and directorship of media organisations.
✦ Attract and retain women in the profession by devising facilities aimed at easing the conflict women journalists face between working conditions and family responsibilities.

Production and programming

✦ Apply gender analysis to programming and develop editorial policies that are gender sensitive and reflect gender equity, so that women's perspectives are equally included.
✦ Provide incentives for creative, gender-sensitive programming in the national media.
✦ Disseminate information on development and social issues in local languages, using traditional, indigenous and other forms of media.
✦ Devise media campaigns that promote gender equality, and provide information aimed at eliminating all forms of violence against women and children.
✦ Target gender-awareness programmes at both women and men.
✦ Sensitise media managers and professionals to increase coverage of women's points of view, especially in political, economic, business and scientific news.
✦ Recognise women as authoritative information sources, experts, and opinion makers – and therefore news sources on any issue.
✦ Introduce, support and extend community radio stations as a way of increasing women's participation and contribution to the media and local economic development.

Outreach and democratisation

✦ Develop and support monitoring bodies and media watch groups that survey media and advertising content concerning gender portrayal.

✦ Include media women in media self-regulatory and other executive committees that draft programme guidelines, budgets, contracts and personnel documents.

✦ Support local, regional, national and international networks for women media professionals and promote co-operation between journalists' organisations, women's professional media associations, women's legal groups and women's political associations.

✦ Develop and/or increase linkages with women's media networks, and assist the financing of these networks.

✦ Advise smaller media, especially those reaching women in rural and marginalised urban areas, on questions such as available technology optimal for their needs.

✦ Interlink grassroots workers and volunteers, media researchers, NGOs, advocacy groups, alternative media networks and policy-makers concerning women and the media.

✦ Create networks of NGOs, women's organisations and professional media organisations with a view to increasing women's participation in media.

✦ Promote public media literacy programmes in order to develop the critical faculties needed for analysing messages disseminated by the media.

✦ Encourage dialogue between the media sector and the field of education in general to raise public awareness of the portrayal of women in the media.

✦ Partner public and private educational institutions to disseminate information about, and increase awareness of women's human rights.

✦ Work in co-operation with journalists' organisations to develop guidelines against gender-biased treatment of information.

✦ Promote dialogue between organisations of journalists and media employers to discuss a joint approach to the ethics of gender portrayal.

Training

✦ Assign programme budgets to allow for women's equal access to all forms of professional training.

✦ Include training modules in gender-awareness, local history and cultural diversity at all media training institutions.

✦ Train women media students and professionals in management and related subjects, such as interpersonal communication and decision-making skills, with a view to promoting women's media enterprises.

✦ Develop train-the-trainer programmes geared specifically for women in computing and all new communications technologies.

✦ Develop educational and training methodologies that enable women's organisations and community groups to effectively communicate their own messages and concerns.

✦ Encourage gender-sensitive training for media professionals to encourage the creation and use of non-stereotyped, balanced and diverse images of women and men in the media.

✦ Sponsor short-term or longer term professional internships or exchanges to expand the professional skills of women media professionals.

Research

✦ Increase research into all aspects of women and media to define areas needing attention and action.

✦ Undertake national studies on media audiences and the impact on viewers of the content of media products. Include the development of follow-up and evaluation systems.

✦ Ensure all national statistics are disaggregated by sex, to facilitate national analysis and planning in the gender mainstreaming process. Aim to repackage research for wide dissemination.

Gender-sensitive action tools

✦ Build and make widely available a database on women working in the media in all fields.

✦ Publish pertinent studies that can assist in building the base for evaluation and planning.

✦ Collect and distribute annual bibliographies on major research activities and findings concerning women in communication and development.

✦ Create a data base of resource materials produced by national women's machineries and women's alternative media networks at local, national, regional and international levels.

✦ Repackage legislation and international conventions on women in simplified forms and in local languages for wide dissemination.

✦ Facilitate the compilation of a Directory of Women Media Experts.

✦ Develop, and maintain with regular updates, a Media Directory of women spokespersons for use by journalists and media practitioners.

✦ Set up an international on-line network for exchange of information on portrayal of women in the media and information on women's media enterprises.

✦ Disseminate non-sexist language guidelines.

✦ Establish, in co-operation with broadcasters, an international video library on women for use in programming and in seminars and workshops aimed at raising gender awareness.

✦ Circulate information sheets on funders interested in the development of communication projects relating to women, alternative media networks, independent women media professionals and NGOs working in popular media forms.

✦ Facilitate the distribution and marketing efforts of women's independent presses and newsletters focusing on women, gender relations and development.

1 Introduction

Scope and Objectives of this Reference Manual

This reference manual provides guidelines for mainstreaming gender into the functions of Ministries of Information and Communication. Its main objective is to assist governments in advancing gender equality in their countries, especially through the establishment and operation of a Gender Management System as a means of mainstreaming gender throughout all government policies, plans, programmes and projects.

The manual examines the major gender issues in the media, communications and development, showing the impetus behind this critical area of concern, its international context, its emancipatory potential and the need for decentralisation. It also provides an overview of existing media policy in Commonwealth regions. While most Commonwealth countries have in place regulatory legislation and/or self-regulatory guidelines and ethical codes governing the media, very few of these instruments mention or deal adequately with gender or address the matter of equal employment opportunities within the sector.

The reference manual describes the current global 'mediascape': who creates, controls and consumes the information presented by the media; what the gender imbalances are in access to and employment in the media; how the marginalisation of women as newsmakers and as subjects of news perpetuates gender inequalities; and how, despite the odds, women have sought to correct these imbalances through alternative media networks.

This manual presents some processes and strategies for mainstreaming gender, and provides an extensive list of recommendations for action, grouped under a series of strategic objectives. It includes a questionnaire for conducting a gender impact analysis as well as tools designed to assist government personnel in putting gender on the agenda of their activities: conducting gender impact analysis, collecting specific data on problems faced by women and men in the sector, using gender-sensitive language, and creating linkages with women's media networks at regional and global levels.

Governments are of course only one of the stakeholders in the information and communications sector. The private sector and civil society organisations play a major role in all aspects of the media, mass communications and information dissemination. To a greater or lesser extent, the activities of these other stakeholders may be beyond the direct control of the government. This manual is aimed at governments, and private-sector and civil society organisations that wish to advance gender equality and equity in the sector. It is designed to present a menu of options and action points that users may adapt to specific circumstances in the national context.

Appendix 1 contains a questionnaire to assist in carrying out a gender impact assessment, and Appendix 2 presents an international and regional listing of women's media associations and networks. Appendix 3 provides a glossary of terms used.

A Gender Framework for the Information Sector

What is gender?

Gender is a concept that refers to a system of roles and relationships between women and men that are determined by the political, economic, social and cultural context rather than by biology. One's biological sex is a natural given; gender, on the other hand, is socially constructed, a "process by which individuals who are born into biological categories of male or female become the social categories of women and men through the acquisition of locally defined attributes of masculinity and femininity" (Kabeer, 1990). In other words, "people are *born* female or male but *learn* to be girls and boys who grow into women and men" (Williams, 1994). We are taught 'appropriate' behaviour and attitudes, roles and activities, expectations and desires. It is this learned behaviour that makes up gender identity and determines gender roles.

The distinction between gender and sex is made to emphasise that everything women and men do, and everything that is expected of them – with the exception of their sexually distinct functions (impregnation; childbearing, breast feeding) varies from one society to another and may change over time according to ideology, culture, religion and economic development (Williams, 1994).

These deeply entrenched attitudes are reflected by the media in their portrayal of women and men as homogenised beings: denying differences, and tending to make invisible or make less of women's contributions in all areas of life at local, national, regional and international levels. Barriteau-Foster (1995) calls for a deconstruction of these received knowledges and frameworks. In order to escape the oppressive relations of gender she suggests a three-step programme of pro-activity to begin reframing perspectives:
1   Acknowledge differences.
2   Recognise the gendered nature of all social relations.
3   Work on the immediate environment to achieve political action.

In some countries and regions, recent gender analysis reveals that in certain areas of life men are disadvantaged, especially young men (for example in educational attainment and and access to health care). Where this occurs, a gendered approach can ensure that interventions address these inequalities appropriately. In most parts of the world, however, it is women who are disadvantaged. Therefore, since this manual is intended to advance gender equality and equity, much of its analysis focuses specifically on ways to improve women's standing in the information sector.

Gender roles

Gender is only one of the ways in which society categorises people. Different roles and characteristics are assigned to people not only on the basis of their gender, but also their race/ethnicity, class/caste, age, religion, disability, or sexual orientation.

How are differentiated gender roles manifested in the social construct and what are the implications for women and men? Four areas are addressed by the *Oxfam Gender Training Manual* (Williams, 1994): work, global resources and benefits, human rights and religion.

In the workplace, women are most often assigned to housekeeping or 'wifely' duties (secretarial work, public relations, cleaning, making coffee), while positions related to finance and management are most often assigned to men. Women tend to have less access to training and other career enhancing opportunities and few provisions are in place that take into account women's triple workload, e.g., flexible working hours, child day-care facilities. Few women are in decision-making positions at all levels.

Resources and benefits are often allocated according to gender, sometimes in an obvious way and at other times, more subtly. In some societies, for example, women are not allowed to own land, so their ability to cultivate (and as a consequence be self-sufficient) depends on a male relative or husband. In others, there may not be any obvious reason why women aren't getting the benefit of, say, literacy classes, but when the issue is examined, one finds women's access is actually limited by their workload and other daily factors impinging on their lives – no time, no energy, no money, no baby-sitter.

Despite the guarantees of equal rights to all people enshrined in the International Declaration on Human Rights, women are routinely denied equal rights to land, property, mobility, education, employment, shelter, food, worship, their children, and the right to manage and care for their own bodies.

While many religions teach equality between people, interpretations of religious texts and traditions can result in women's subordination, and in practice women often play a subordinate role or are excluded altogether from the religious decision-making hierarchy. Nonetheless, for many women, religion continues to be a great source of hope and support. Likewise, while many culturally sanctioned practices – such as genital mutilation and preferential feeding of male children – damage women and make their lives difficult and painful, culture can be a source of cohesion and solidarity among women and between women and men. The challenge lies in changing discriminatory practices for both women and men, while retaining the positive attributes of particular cultures.

Journalists and media managers are just as subject to these influences as other members of society. These influences are all-pervasive and include "the individual journalist's skills and values, the written and unwritten rules of the profession, the dynamics of the particular newsroom, the organisational culture and structure of the media organisation – its aims and objectives, competition in the media market, the negotiating of interest groups – each with their own intentions, legal constraints, audience expectations ..." (de Bruin, 1995).

Content is determined on subjective factors that often skew the information broadcast or printed. The fact is that journalists and journalism not only "reflect society but also affect the society of which they are a part ... overtly, through editorials and commentaries and, less obviously, in terms of story choices, angles and so on ..." (Francis-Brown, 1995).

Communicating gender

Objectivity is often held up as the main principle of journalism. Traditionally, objectivity has been defined by the mainstream media as truth in its purest sense: truth uncoloured by feelings and opinions. But how does the assumption of objectivity find expression by individual communicators socialised into accepting unequal relationships between men and women as the norm? Once this reality is clear, the importance of raising gender awareness among writers, reporters, editors and all those involved in the creative process, becomes self-evident.

The critical areas to target are:

Language: The UNESCO guidelines on non-sexist language are aimed at giving fair treatment to individuals and groups by assisting authors and editors to "avoid writing in a manner that reinforces questionable attitudes and assumptions about people and sex roles." There is little extra work or difficulty involved in being language conscious, merely a requirement that editors examine current conventions and substitute more precise meanings that respect the way people wish to be viewed. For example: former 'blacks' in the US are now 'African-Americans'; the 'handicapped' are now the 'disabled'; 'Ms' has become the female equivalent of 'Mr' since neither indicates marital status.

Stereotyping: Women are too often tagged with stereotypical labels, e.g., 'mother of three', 'the wife of so and so' (as though these were the only relevant facts about the person); or labelled as 'feminist' in a code that suggests the subject is not acting according to traditional gender roles, and that this is in some way a 'bad' thing; a woman Member of Parliament or in some other position of influence will have her clothes and hair described in minute detail, while her male colleagues are distinguished by achievements unrelated to their physical appearance. Defining women in terms of their appearance, or offering excuses for their political opinions, delegitimises their achievements, and renders them less threatening and more palatable to the status quo.

Men too can be portrayed by the media in stereotypically negative ways, "... as rarely to be trusted ... as completely evil ... [or] as stupid buffoons. Even male heroes are often given one-sided and simplified characterisations" (Jackins et al, 1999).

Story selection: Many good stories about women are never told because they are not given any importance, or because there is no conscious effort to find out what women are doing or what their views are on, say, financing or engineering or football.

Communicating gender requires journalists and other media practitioners to observe the ways that people may be marginalised because of their gender as well as race/ethnicity, class/caste, age and other such factors. Who gets coverage? From what perspective? Through which lens? Reflecting which stereotypes about people from different gender, race/ethnic, class/caste, and other groups? Are stories helping to advance gender equality and equity in society or are they angled in a way that upholds traditional attitudes and values? Are women's or men's concerns being separated from the concerns of society in general?

Gender and development

The belief in the possibility of change for the better is the essence of development work, yet development planners and policy-makers are often unwilling, or unable, to recognise the role that gender plays in the outcome of initiatives and interventions. One difficulty in introducing gender concerns into development planning has been the perception that gender is a subject for scholars, specialists or, simply, women. "Many attitudes expressed by development workers at the community, national and international level demonstrate a gap between gender concepts as discussed by experts and application of these concerns in policies, programmes and day-to-day work" (Shallat and Paredes, 1995). Perceptions about appropriate behaviours for women and men are deeply embedded and false assumptions and stereotypes taken as axiomatic – thus 'hard' news (politics, war, economics, etc.) becomes the domain of male journalists, and 'soft' news (social issues, environment, etc.) becomes that of female journalists.

Another element that often escapes development workers is the essential role of the media in advancing development, not merely for their publicity value but as meaningful components of projects (Shallat and Paredes, 1995). Media and communications have been important components in community development, playing an essential part in helping to change the deeply entrenched values that place women in a subordinate position to men. Community media and people-to-people communication (as opposed to the top-down packages offered by the mainstream media) inform, educate, and empower using local languages and cultural norms and practices.

Gender on the Global Agenda

"Everywhere the potential exists for the media to make a far greater contribution to the advancement of women ...."

Beijing Platform for Action

Women and the media is a Critical Area of Concern (Section J, paragraphs 234-245) in the Platform for Action, the final document signed by 187 governments – including all Commonwealth governments – at the United Nations Fourth World Conference on Women held in Beijing in September 1995. Section J outlines actions to be taken by governments, national and international media, non-governmental organisations (NGOs) and media professionals around two strategic objectives:

1   Increasing women's participation and access to expression and decision-making in and through the media and new technologies of communication. Here the actions relate to women's education, training and employment; women's participation in drawing up policy, developing non-stereotypical programming, and in the new information technologies, and strengthening women's media networks.

2   Promoting a balanced and non-stereotyped portrayal of women and girls in the media; encouraging gender-sensitive training for media professionals; and taking effective measures against pornography.

It could be said that Section J has been in the making for the past 20 years. The current development discourse on gender and media began in the decade of the seventies within the framework of three international events and processes: the United Nations Decade for Women (1976-1985), the New International Information and Communication Order (NIICO) spearheaded by UNESCO, and the networking activities of women's movements worldwide.

The aim of the UN Decade for Women, which followed the 1975 International Women's Year Conference (Mexico City),[1] was to focus attention on the "systematic nature of discrimination against women ..." (Gallagher, 1994). The main goal of the NIICO was "to correct the imbalance of information and communication between the North and South and the lack of it South to South ..." (Anand, 1994). The NIICO recommendations were mainly addressed to the larger international news agencies and only a small part of the initiative addressed the absence of women's voices in mainstream media.

At the same time, women's movements, particularly in the South but also in the North, were gaining momentum; networking regionally and internationally and exchanging information through newsletters, bulletins and by word of mouth: "small, lightweight media, folk media and interpersonal communications (which) were most appropriate for reaching the masses of women in developing countries" (Adagala and Kiai, 1994). Women's media networks and women's studies programmes took the lead in gender research, analysis and action with regard to media content and employment patterns.

Further activity by women's media networks, UNESCO and concerned media activists prior to the Fourth World Conference on Women was instrumental in ensuring the inclusion of women's media concerns in the Platform for Action. Issues raised in a number of documents produced in international meetings of women working at all levels of the information and communication sector are reflected in the Beijing Platform. These documents speak of the essential need "to promote forms of communication that not only challenge the patriarchal nature of media but strive to decentralise and democratise them; to create media that encourage dialogue and debate, media that advance women's and peoples' creativity, media that reaffirm women's wisdom and knowledge, and that make people into subjects rather than objects or targets of communication, media which are responsive to peoples needs" (Bangkok Declaration, 1994).

While it is acknowledged that information technologies create new opportunities for women to participate in communications and media, and for the dissemination of information that can advance gender equality and equity, the documents recognise the imbalance of information flows from North to South that can have a negative impact on existing cultures and values in the receiver countries.

These documents also recognise that a greater involvement by women in both the technical and decision-making areas of communication and media would increase awareness of women's lives from their own perspectives. Since women are concerned with the basic needs of their communities and the environment, these documents argue, promoting women's interests in particular, in fact serves the interests of all humanity. They each call for significant support to enable women to create progressive change.

In its forward-looking strategies, the Platform for Action suggests that "women should be empowered by enhancing their skills, knowledge and access to information technology. This will strengthen their ability to combat negative portrayals of women internationally and to challenge instances of abuse of the power of an increasingly important industry" (paragraph 237).

The 1995 Commonwealth Plan of Action on Gender and Development includes 15 action points that are recommended for governments to take in order to advance gender equality and equity. These action points include the following:

✦ **undertake an advocacy role in partnership with the media:** support gender training for journalists in order to ensure broad and non-discriminatory representation of women in the media and advertising, and encourage reporting on women's achievements, difficulties and multiple roles; and

✦ **use gender-sensitive and gender-inclusive language:** use gender-inclusive language in legislation, government documents and all educational materials, and promote its use in the mass media.

A consultative approach is required in mapping out actions to be taken by all the actors – governments, regulators, broadcasters, and civil society, particularly women engaged in creating and fostering alternative media that seek to make information available to all, and who promote communication as a participatory exercise. Such an approach, particularly with respect to the sensitive area of media content, fosters the development of democratic practices and offers broader possibilities for freedom of expression in civil society.

Regional Policy Perspectives

Freedom of expression is a concept deeply embedded in most media organisations and is accompanied by a tradition of resistance to anything perceived as an attempt to influence output – however well-intentioned that effort may be. Nonetheless, many countries have in place some form of legislation or guidelines which seek to direct or encourage ethical behaviour on the part of the media, although these typically cover broadcasting services rather than the print media. Specific language in respect to gender – either stereotyping or employment practices – is less apparent. The effectiveness of such regulation and/or legislation, by themselves, is a matter of some debate. It is often argued that both the content and the effectiveness of legislation and/or guidelines is enhanced where watchdog groups are at their most active in lobbying the media and raising public awareness.

Africa

In Africa, the most significant change in the past two decades has been a trend towards allowing private broadcasting stations to come into co-existence with state-controlled networks which previously held a monopoly. In most countries censorship boards exist within broadcasting organisations and national film distribution organisations. In general these boards attempt to minimise the screening of excessive violence, explicit sexual scenes, politically undesirable material and anything else deemed as culturally offensive. But these boards tend to be male-dominated and gender-related issues are not explicitly addressed. National communication policies, where they exist, do not appear to address gender (Adagala and Kiai, 1994).

Asia/Pacific

In Asia/Pacific during the same period, the trend has been towards establishing self-regulatory mechanisms and providing guidelines rather than enacting laws. One such example is *Australia's Fair Exposure Guidelines;* first developed in 1993 by the Government's Office of Multicultural Affairs, it has since been updated by the Status of Women Office. However, few other Asian or Pacific countries have guidelines, regulatory mechanisms or affirmative action policies aimed specifically at advancing gender equality.

India has in place an Indecent Representation of Women (Prohibition) Act, passed by the Indian parliament in 1986 which, "prohibits indecent representation of women through advertisements or in publications, writings, paintings, figures or in any other manner." The punishment imposed for violation is a fine and up to five years' imprisonment. The Act was based on the recommendations of a 60-member committee on the Portrayal of Women in the Media, constituted in 1983. After passage of the Bill, a smaller advisory committee was constituted to oversee its implementation in October 1987. But in Asia, citizen initiatives are generally the most effective. These include the Tokyo-based Forum for Citizen's Television, which developed a list of Television Viewers' Rights that has helped raise awareness and indirectly influenced programming and advertising norms (Balakrishnan, 1994).

Canada and the Caribbean

In Canada, women have done much to improve the portrayal of women, increase women's presence in broadcasting and facilitate the communication of women's perspectives. Over several years, the Toronto-based NGO National Watch on Images of Women in the Media (MediaWatch) Inc. and the National Action Committee on the Status of Women, comprising hundreds of women's organisations, helped bring about the final passage of provision 3.(1) (c) of the Broadcasting Act, which states:

"the Canadian broadcasting system should through its programming and the employment opportunities arising out of its operations, serve the needs and interests, and reflect the circumstances and aspirations, of Canadian men, women and children, including equal rights, the linguistic duality and multicultural nature of Canadian society and the special place of aboriginal peoples within the society."

and:

"the programming provided by the Canadian broadcasting system should be varied and comprehensive, providing balance of information, enlightenment and entertainment for men and women of all ages, interests and tastes."

Observation of the fair portrayal and employment requirements of the Broadcasting Act is a "condition of license" for the publicly owned Canadian Broadcasting Corporation (CBC) and the privately owned broadcast stations of the Canadian Association of Broadcasters. CBC also has its own Employment Equity Office and an Equitable Portrayal Office and it reports to the Canadian Radio and Television and Telecommunications Commission (CRTC) periodically on the progress of women and minorities in various categories. Its guidelines seek to avoid sex role stereotyping and sexist language, reflect women and their interests in news reporting and public affairs, recognise the full participation of women in Canadian life and seek out women's opinions. But, according to the literature, in practice the CRTC does little reinforcement and has never denied a broadcast license or renewal on the grounds of violations of the Broadcasting Act or any of its guidelines.

In the Caribbean, it is only recently that women's employment in the media and the media's portrayal of women have emerged as subject areas for specialised enquiry. Legislation governing the operations of the mass media exists only in the larger countries – Barbados, Jamaica, and Trinidad and Tobago – and then only in respect of broadcasting services. The print media are subject to the laws of libel which apply to all areas of social activity. Even where legislation exists, it is silent on gender. Caribbean Community (CARICOM) information ministers adopted a policy on communication and culture in the region, but this too makes no mention of gender issues and concerns. National and regional bodies concerned with content (professional associations, advertising standards councils, etc.) tend to emphasise self-regulation, enjoining members to refrain from making offensive references on the basis of race, sex, nationality, religion or ideology. Media houses have rarely written editorial policies that are gender specific (Wallace, 1994).

Western Europe

In Western Europe, media institutions have traditionally followed a system of self-regulation with relatively few formal directives or legislative constraints apart from basic and fairly general requirements to respect standards of decency and good taste, the latter usually within the context of the protection of minors. The 1989 European Directive on Television Broadcasting only includes one reference relevant to the portrayal of women which concerns television advertising which, it states, must not "include any discrimination on grounds of race, sex or nationality" (Article 2b). Legislation at the national level is extremely general in nature and few media organisations have any additional guidelines or policies (Gallagher, 1994). The situation is more clearly defined in respect of employment practices. In the UK, for example, the Independent Television Commission is empowered (by the 1990 Broadcasting Act) to grant and renew licenses on condition of "equality of opportunity between men and women" (Article 108). Nevertheless, largely as a result of activism by women's organisations, the media have opened up significantly to the articulation of women's voices, perspectives and concerns.

Notes

1 Follow-up conferences were held in 1980 (Copenhagen, Denmark), 1985 (Nairobi, Kenya), and 1995 (Beijing, China).

2 These include The Bangkok Declaration from the Women Empowering Media Conference held in Bangkok, Thailand in February, 1994 (World Association for Christian Communications, Isis Manila and the International Women's Tribune Centre); the Toronto Platform for Action from the UNESCO International Symposium on "Women and the Media: Access to Expression and Decision-Making" held in Toronto, Canada in March 1995; and reports from the Regional NGO Meetings in the Pacific, Latin America and the Caribbean, Africa and the Middle East, and Europe and North America in the process leading up to the Beijing conference; the Dublin Meeting of Women Broadcasters for Beijing held in June 1995; and the International Women and Media Seminar convened in Kalmar, Sweden, in June 1995.

2 Gender Mainstreaming

What is Gender Mainstreaming?

Gender mainstreaming means integrating a gender equality perspective into all the mainstream activities of government, at the policy, programme and project levels. It involves:

✦ forging and strengthening the political will to achieve gender equality and equity, at the local, national, regional and global levels;

✦ incorporating a gender perspective into the planning processes of all ministries and departments of government, particularly those concerned with macroeconomic and development planning, personnel policies and management, and legal and constitutional affairs including the administration of justice;

✦ integrating a gender perspective into sectoral planning cycles, including the analysis, development, appraisal, implementation, monitoring and evaluation of policies, programmes and projects;

✦ using sex-disaggregated data in statistical analysis to reveal how policies impact differently on women and men;

✦ increasing the numbers of women in decision-making positions in government, and the public and private sectors;

✦ providing tools and training in gender analysis and gender planning to decision-makers, senior managers and other key personnel to ensure that they know how to integrate a gender perspective into their work; and

✦ forging linkages between governments, the private sector, civil society and other stakeholders to ensure a co-ordination of efforts and resources.

Background

The strategy of mainstreaming has evolved out of efforts by the international women's movement to change the attitudes, assumptions, working practices and activities of public institutions which reproduce and contribute to gender inequalities.

Since the 1970s, women have called on international development agencies and governments to 'integrate' women into the developmental process. An early institutional response was the establishment of Women's Bureaux and departments which funded, targeted, or took part in a variety of women's projects. But progress was slow and there was little improvement in women's status and wellbeing while women-specific projects remained marginalised. Devoid of a fundamental reorientation of dominant gender stereotypes, this approach actually served to increase women's workloads and reinforce gender inequalities.

It was in this context in the mid-1980s that the gender and development (GAD) approach gained currency. Within institutions, the GAD approach seeks to base interventions on the analysis of women's and men's roles and needs in order to correct inequalities and inequities. Among other things, this approach promotes a more equitable distribution of power and decision-making. According to Kabeer (1996) there are three levels of institutional power which should be taken into consideration in the mainstreaming approach:

1 Power that allows each individual to influence decisions in the direction s/he desires.
2 Power that prevents issues which are not in the interests of power holders from being placed on the agenda.
3 Power which inhibits articulation of conflicts since both the subordinate and dominant groups are unaware of the oppressive implications, or are incapable of imagining alternative ways of being and doing.

For the exercise to succeed, the aim should be to allow each individual to influence decisions. If power holders block discussion of issues outside their interests, and/or inhibit articulation by those without power the process of gender mainstreaming cannot work effectively.

Policy Approaches

A further distinction can be made between an 'integrationist' and an 'agenda-setting' approach to mainstreaming. The first merely aims to integrate women's concerns into existing development activities without necessarily altering the agenda, while the second attempts to transform the thrust of development policy as it brings women's concerns into the mainstream. Kabeer (1996) has identified three possible approaches to policy:

✦ Gender-neutral policies are those that are seen as having no significant gender dimension. However, government policies seldom if ever have the same effect on women as they do on men, even if at first sight they may appear to exist in a context where gender is irrelevant. Thus policies which may appear to be 'gender-neutral' are often in fact 'gender-blind', and are biased in favour of males because they presuppose that those involved in and affected by the policy are males, with male needs and interests.
✦ Gender-specific policies take into account gender differentials, and target women or men specifically, but leave the current distribution of resources and responsibilities intact.
✦ Gender-aware/redistributive/transformative policies seek to transform existing gender relations by changing the distribution of resources and responsibilities to make it more equitable. These policies are the most politically challenging, because they involve altering the existing balance of power between men and women, but they also go the furthest towards addressing not only practical gender needs but strategic gender interests as well (adapted from Kabeer, 1996).

The basic choice presented here is whether media policy reflects, perpetuates, or challenges gender hierarchies. The latter approach involves the implementation of gender-transformative policies and implies a proactive effort to avoid stereotyping; ensure the equal participation of women and men role in decision-making, agenda-setting and content-determining activities; and advance gender equality on all fronts.

The depth of gender stereotyping among all those involved in the information and communications process needs to be both openly acknowledged and acted upon – training, guidelines and processes need to be established to counteract and break down these attitudes. Varying degrees of resistance can be expected – from power-holders as well as those who are subordinated. Resistance can even come from those who have been working on women in development (WID) issues, if they feel that gender and development issues will supersede WID in the ministry's action agenda (Kabeer, 1990; Moser, 1993; Razavi and Miller, 1995).

Even though gender relations are always present, taking them into account requires a special interest in seeking them out. This involves asking a number of searching questions:

✦ To what extent does the media environment (decision-making, programming, editorial policy, employment and assignment practices) reflect the needs, interests and voices of women in fair proportion to that of men?
✦ Are policy-makers, reporters and editors armed with the knowledge and awareness that is required to advance gender equality and equity in and through the media?
✦ Are there guidelines, staffing and financial resources in place to enable them to develop and implement policies to promote gender equality in copy and on equal access to expression and participation in the media?
✦ Is there 'space' for both women and men to pursue their media careers?
✦ Are gender relations monitored when women head the production team?[1]

The task requires clear political will and the allocation of additional human and financial resources as needed. The government ministry responsible for information and (tele)communication may give responsibility for the gender mainstreaming task to a specific team or group of persons but care must be taken to ensure that these persons have the authority and/or seniority to adequately promote a gender-aware perspective among staff in general and senior management in particular. Benchmarks should be established and concrete work plans drawn up in respect to actions, mechanisms and processes throughout the system. A credible monitoring mechanism should be in place, as should standards of accountability.

An understanding of the concept of gender should not be assumed. Steps should be taken to raise awareness among all levels of staff including the introduction of non-sexist language guidelines and gender-aware editorial practices. Unless staff at all levels feel they have a stake in the exercise and unless action is taken to encourage their participation, involvement will be unlikely to go beyond the small circle of staff with direct responsibility. Women should be targeted by creating spaces for them to freely articulate their specific needs and concerns.

The Roles and Responsibilities of the Ministry

The government ministry responsible for the information and (tele)communications sector is assumed to have the following functions in relation to the media:

1 Policy analysis and development
2 Policy-making at the political/ministerial level
3 Administration and implementation of policy (policy deployment)
4 Regulation
5 Government information and media services

Gender is a cross-cutting theme that should extend across the entire gamut of the system. Ministries of Information and Communication have a key role to play in this process, including raising awareness of gender considerations within government sector programming and to the broader society. Within the government, two key areas to link with are the education sector and national women's machineries. Within civil society linkages should be forged with the private sector media, professional media bodies, women's development NGOs, and alternative media networks.

The Gender Management System

The Gender Management System (GMS)is an approach to gender mainstreaming developed by the Commonwealth. The GMS is an integrated network of structures, mechanisms and processes designed to make government more gender-aware; increase the numbers of women in decision-making positions within and outside government; facilitate the formulation of gender-sensitive policies, plans and programmes; and promote the advancement of gender equality and equity in society.

Figure 1   **The Gender Management System (GMS)**

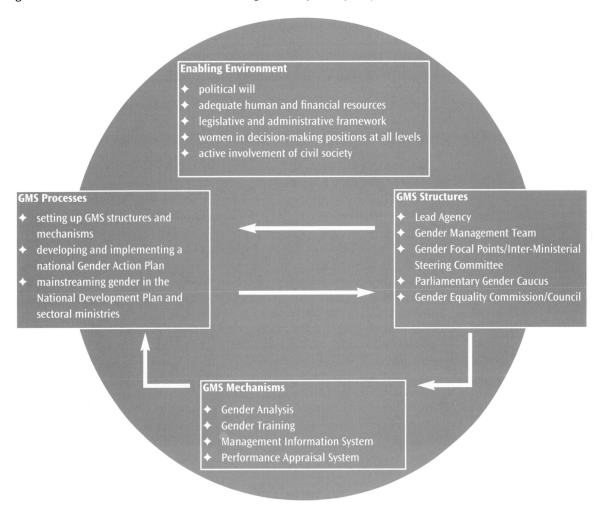

The enabling environment of a GMS

The establishment and operation of a Gender Management System requires an enabling environment. There are a number of interrelated factors that determine the degree to which the environment in which the GMS is being set up does or does not enable effective gender mainstreaming. These enabling factors include the following:

+ political will and commitment to gender equality at the highest levels;
+ global and regional mandates such as CEDAW, the Beijing Platform for Action, and the Commonwealth Plan of Action.
+ adequate human and financial resources;
+ a legislative and constitutional framework that is conducive to advancing gender equality;
+ the presence of a critical mass of women in decision-making roles;
+ civil society and the role it can play in advancing gender equality; and
+ donor aid and technical assistance, such as that provided by the Commonwealth and other international agencies.

GMS structures and mechanisms

The GMS puts forward the following structures to facilitate gender mainstreaming (Commonwealth Secretariat, 1999):

+ a **Lead Agency** (usually the Ministry of Gender or Women's Affairs or other National Women's Machinery), which initiates and strengthens the GMS institutional arrangements, provides overall co-ordination and monitoring, and carries out advocacy, communications, media relations, and reporting;

+ a **Gender Management Team** (consisting of representatives from the Lead Agency, key government ministries and civil society), which provides leadership for the implementation of the GMS; defines broad operational policies, indicators of effectiveness, and timeframes for implementation; and monitors its performance;

+ an **Inter-Ministerial Steering Committee** whose members are representatives of the Lead Agency and the Gender Focal Points (see below) of all government ministries, and which ensures that gender mainstreaming in government policy, planning and programmes in all sectors is effected and that strong linkages are established between ministries;

+ **Gender Focal Points** (senior administrative and technical staff in all government ministries), who co-ordinate gender activities (e.g., training), promote gender mainstreaming in the planning, implementation and evaluation of all activities in their respective sectors, and sit on the Inter-Ministerial Steering Committee;

+ a **Parliamentary Gender Caucus** (consisting of gender-aware female and male parliamentarians), which carries out awareness raising, lobbying, and promoting the equal participation of women and men in politics and all aspects of national life, and brings a gender perspective to bear on parliamentary structures and procedures, and matters under debate;

+ representatives of **civil society** (a National Gender Equality Commission/Council, academic institutions, NGOs, professional associations, media and other stakeholders), who represent and advocate the interests and perspectives of autonomous associations in government policy-making and implementation processes.

Mechanisms for advancing gender equality in the context of a GMS include the following:

+ **Gender analysis:** This involves the collection and analysis of sex-disaggregated data which reveals the differential impact of development activities on women and men, and the effect gender roles and responsibilities have on development efforts. It also involves qualitative analyses that help to clarify how and why these differential, roles, responsibilities and impacts have come about.

+ **Gender training:** many of the stakeholders in a GMS will require training in such areas as basic gender awareness and sensitisation, gender analysis, gender planning, the use of gender-sensitive indicators, and monitoring and evaluation. Since the GMS aims at the gradual transformation of organisations and a realignment of the belief systems, power structures, and policy and planning processes within them, training may also be required in conflict prevention and resolution, and the management of change.

+ **Management Information System:** this is the mechanism for gathering the data necessary for gender analysis, and sharing and communicating the findings of that analysis, using sex-disaggregated data and gender-sensitive indicators. The Management Information System is much more than just a library or resource centre; it is the central repository of gender information and the means by which such information is generated by and disseminated to the key stakeholders in the GMS.

✦ **Performance Appraisal System:** based on the results of gender analysis, the GMS should establish targets in specific areas. The achievement of these targets should be evaluated both at the individual and departmental level, through a gender-aware Performance Appraisal System. This should not be separate from whatever system is already in place for appraising the performance of employees – rather the present system should be reviewed to ensure that it is gender-sensitive. The Performance Appraisal System should also take into account the level of gender sensitivity and skills (e.g., as acquired through gender training or field experience) of individuals. The Gender Management Team should work in partnership with the central personnel office of government and sectoral personnel departments to ensure that the Performance Appraisal System in place reflects these concerns (Commonwealth Secretariat, 1999).

GMS processes

The processes involved in implementing a Gender Management System include developing and implementing a national Gender Action Plan, which should include provisions for setting up or strengthening the GMS structures and mechanisms, and for engendering core ministries and sectoral policy and planning. Normally spearheaded by the Ministry of Women's Affairs or other national women's machinery, the Gender Action Plan should include specific guidelines for setting up Gender Focal Points and mainstreaming gender into the regular policy, planning and implementation cycles of the Ministry of Information and Communications. These cycles have five main phases, and a gender perspective needs to be integrated in each phase:

1 **Gender analysis:** this involves analysing the status of women vis-à-vis men in the sector and examining the impact on women and men of information and communications policy.

2 **Policy development and appraisal:** establishing gender priorities according to individual national circumstances, developing policy options to address gender imbalances, and appraising options to determine their gender impact.

3 **Gender-aware action plans:** the output of policy development is a plan which should have a clearly defined gender dimension.

4 **Implementation:** the implementation of the engendered work plan takes place as part of the normal functioning of government.

5 **Monitoring and Evaluation:** this involves reviewing key indicators on the status of women in the national context in the sector, and feeding the findings into the next planning cycle.

Notes

1   Exchanging one gender role for another is not in itself a sign of gender awareness. "Men and women can do different types of jobs and be equal, and they can do the same kind of job and be unequal. What matters is not so much who does what, but rather who defines the role of the other, and whether both women and men have a choice" (Farr and Chitiga, 1991).

3 Gender and the Media

The Media Market

During the past two decades there has been an explosion in the field of information technology which has in turn spawned a global communication network that transcends national boundaries and impacts on public policy. "With advances in computer technology and satellite and cable TV, global access to information – although this is not always used democratically – continues to increase and expand, creating new opportunities for the participation of women in communications and media and for dissemination of information about women ..." (Toronto Platform for Action, UNESCO, 1995).

Today's media can deliver messages and symbols – imported or domestic – directly into almost every home. Unfortunately, however, they continue to perpetuate and reinforce negative, stereotypical images of both women and men, according to which the resort to violence on the part of some males is presented as a 'natural' and acceptable way of resolving conflicts, and which do not provide an accurate or realistic picture of women's multiple roles and contributions to an ever-changing world.

Additionally, it is an increasingly centralised industry, as the resources in this profit-driven global media market have become concentrated in fewer and fewer hands. In 1993, for instance, Rupert Murdoch's News Corporation acquired a majority interest in Star Television, based in Hong Kong, thereby making it the largest satellite broadcasting empire in the world.[1]

"Western wire services dominate news coverage" (Steeves, 1990) and at both global and regional levels, "the shift to high technology ... has widened differences in technical resources, skills and capabilities among countries" (Adagala and Kiai, 1994). Gallagher (1994) speaks of "the transnationalisation of the women's magazine industry in Europe."

But while these developments give the impression of a world swamped by information and communications technologies emanating from a few Western sources, the fact is that millions of women across the globe remain untouched by the mass media: they do not have the time, access or literacy skills to pursue information and/or news (Gallagher, 1995).

Audience

The mass media are major socialising agents in modern society. Where media systems are highly developed, people spend at least four hours a day watching television, listening to radio and reading magazines and newspapers. Although in domestic viewing and listening situations, the decisions of the adult male in the household tend to prevail (Mytton, 1993; Lull, 1988), women are enthusiastic media users.

The pattern of preferences is similar worldwide: men prefer sports, action-oriented programmes and information (especially news); women prefer popular drama, music, dance and other entertainment programmes (Sepstrup and Goonasekara, 1994; Bonder and Zurutuza, 1993). Numerous studies worldwide have established that by far the favourite television genre among women is serialised drama, soap opera and telenovelas because of the exceptionally high proportion of female characters in such programmes (Brown, 1990; Seiter et al, 1989; Lull, 1988). Media content which features powerful, dynamic male characters and in which women play decorative, supportive roles (as in action drama), or which revolve almost exclusively around male figures (as in most sports and news programming), appeals primarily to men. This is not to suggest that all men or women prefer these categories of programmes, simply that this is the dominant trend observed by the researchers.

Access

Gender differences are linked to power and influence in the mainstream media. Over 400 women communicators from 80 countries called the media "a male-dominated tool used by those in power" (Bangkok Declaration, 1994). Hosken (1996) asks the question, "Who is sending messages to whom and therefore making decisions for all involved?" and makes it clear in her answer that "international communication and the tools used are almost exclusively male prerogatives." According to a 1995 global survey (Global Media Monitoring Project), "It is evident that gender differences are linked to power and influence," and "news gathering and news reporting are rooted in a value system which accords higher status to men and 'the masculine'." The way the world is portrayed on television "serves to maintain entrenched power imbalances," and "this fits into a long history of the use of public displays of violence to maintain rankings of domination ..." (Eisler, 1996).

Overall, news, for example, is increasingly being presented *by* women but it is still very rarely *about* women. According to the 1995 Global Media Monitoring Project,[2] women comprised 43 percent of journalists but only 17 per cent of those interviewed as experts or opinion makers (see Tables 1 and 2). The largest number of males interviewed (29 per cent) appeared in stories on politics and government, while the largest proportion of female interviewees appeared in stories on disasters/accidents (20 per cent) and on crime (17 per cent). On a global level female reporters cover stories categorised as 'other' stories (arts, entertainment, environment, pollution, health, housing, human rights, science and social issues) while men covered 'core' stories (crime, disasters, economy, international crises, labour, national defence, politics and government).

Studies in Germany and the United Kingdom suggest that the presence of more women journalists and female experts voicing opinions in the media would create "significant role models for other women, stimulate female interest in public issues, and – perhaps – sometimes speak in the interests of and for women" (Sreberny-Mohammadi, 1994).

Another solution is for the media to shift attention away from the traditional 'power' perspectives with respect to the top echelons of politics, government and business, and focus more on aspects that are more inclusive of women. This is not to suggest an abandonment of power and influence, but rather that the media broaden their horizons and seek greater inclusiveness and diversity in their reporting. A feature on, say, a general election can speak to the (mainly male) candidates but it can also examine women's involvement as candidates, polling clerks, scrutineers and in other positions that actually make the event happen. It can also ask pertinent questions: what are the barriers to women running for office? What do women get out of all this when their party comes to power? In the case of business, stories can seek to make visible women's contributions to the GNP of a country – as small farmers, entrepreneurs, and through their (often unpaid) domestic work.

Employment Patterns

During International Women's Year (1995), when world attention was focused on the systematic nature of discrimination against women, "things seemed deceptively simple: if more women worked in the media, it was said, the media would change for the better" (Gallagher, 1994).

Since then, most regions have seen a steady growth in the numbers, range and scope of women working in mainstream media, but women are much more likely to be concentrated in administrative than in the other occupational categories (i.e., production/editorial, design, and technical). Of all the women working in media, some 50 per cent are located in administration in contrast to five per cent on average in the technical field (see Table 2) (Gallagher and von Euler, 1995).

Women still lack the power to develop media policy, or to determine the nature and shape of media content. This is so even in North America, where a dramatic increase has been noted in women-owned media and in women's organisations working on media representation issues. According to National Federation of Press Women (USA) figures, women increased their share of management posts by only one per cent per year between 1977 and 1993 and if that trend were to continue it would be another 30 years before gender balance is attained in newspaper jobs in the US (NFPW, 1993). A 1995 survey by the US-based International Women's Media Foundation states: "the news media remains an industry dominated and directed by men." In Europe, "in every professional category women are disproportionately situated in the lower salary bands and the less authoritative jobs" (Gallagher, 1994). In Africa, "on the average, women represent less than 20 per cent of workers in media organisations (and) lack influence where it really matters" (Adagala and Kiai, 1994).

"The very top jobs in media – director general, chief executive, president – are almost exclusively occupied by men," according to a 1995 UNESCO study of gender patterns in media employment spanning 43 countries (Gallagher and von Euler, 1995). Of 239 media organisations studied, only eight (3 per cent) were headed by women. Another eight, mostly small radio companies or news magazines, had female deputy directors.

Women's average share of posts at the top three levels of management is below 20 per cent in all media and all regions except for broadcasting in Latin America. "While it is heartening to see that some women can and do succeed in reaching the summit of media management ... these women represent a tiny proportion of all women working in the media. Analysis of European broadcasting data shows that, at the top level of the management hierarchy can be found one in every 1,000 female employees and one in every 140 male employees. On average, men are seven times more likely than women to reach the top" (Gallagher and von Euler, 1995).

Women are a minority in the committees and boards that define and shape policy, holding just 12 per cent of these positions in broadcasting, and nine per cent in the press. Of the 120 top management committees in radio and television worldwide, more than half (67) include no women at all. In the press just under half (21) of the 45 equivalent committees have no women. Women do slightly better in terms of seats

Table 1

Proportion of Female/Male Journalists Against Female/Male Actors in Main Subject Areas by Region

Africa

Proportion of female and male journalists in main subject areas

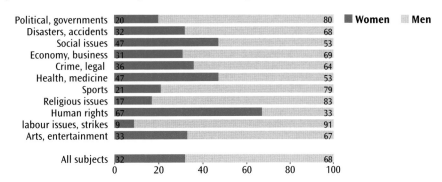

Proportion of female and male news actors in main subject areas

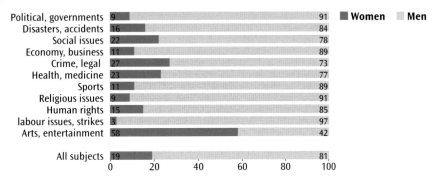

Asia

Proportion of female and male journalists in main subject areas

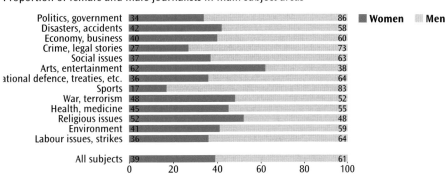

Proportion of female and male news actors in main subject areas

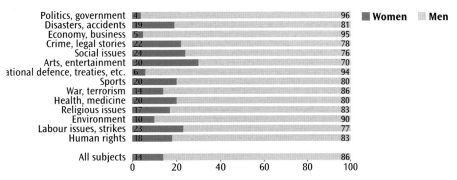

The Carribean and Central America

Proportion of female and male journalists in main subject areas

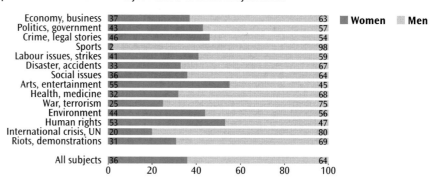

Proportion of female and male news actors in main subject areas

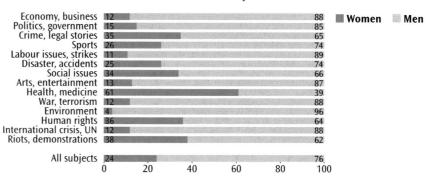

The Pacific

Proportion of female and male journalists in main subject areas

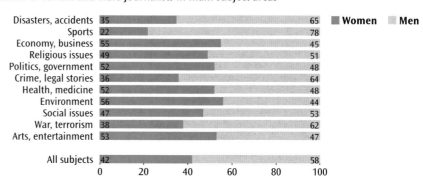

Proportion of female and male news actors in main subject areas

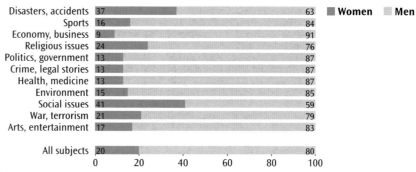

Source: Women's Participation in the News, WACC 1996

Table 2 **Presence of Women and Men in Newspapers, Radio & Television by Region**

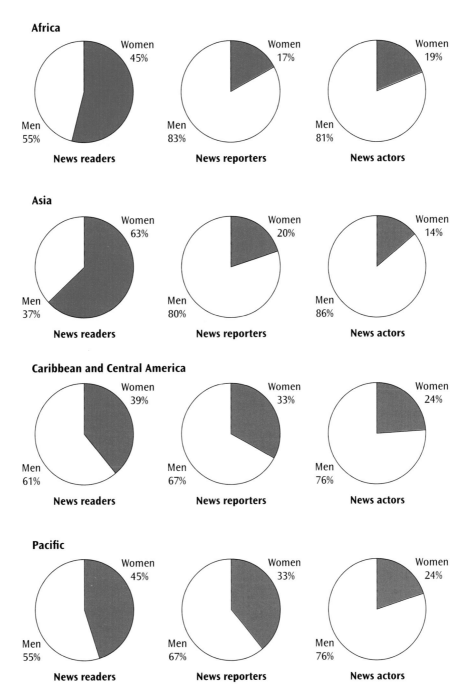

Source: Women's Participation in the News, WACC 1996

Table 3

Women's and men's overall share of jobs in main occupational categories, broadcasting

Production

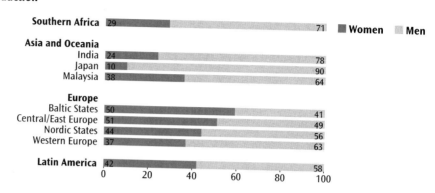

Crafts

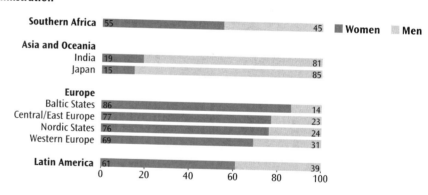

Administration

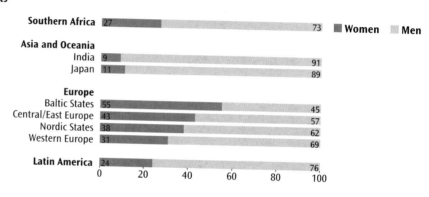

Technical

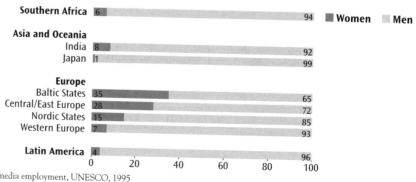

Source: An unfinished story: Gender patterns in media employment, UNESCO, 1995

on governing boards, the external bodies which advise broadcasting organisations on policy and, in some cases, on financial matters – although these vary considerably in influence from one organisation to another. In broadcasting, 16 per cent of board members are women; and in the press, 21 per cent. However, about 30 per cent of these governing bodies have no female members: 32 of the 105 boards in broadcasting, and nine of the 31 boards in the press include no women at all.

Despite the general upward trend in their numbers and visibility women also drop out at a greater rate than men. The most commonly reported obstacle to career development reported by women is that of male attitudes. Women are constantly judged by male standards and performance criteria of what constitutes news and who constitutes a newsmaker, a gender bias which leads to discrimination in the awarding of assignments: many women journalists report being denied approval to cover beats such as science and technology, politics and economics.

Women are also confronted by social disapproval since the critical, independent, assertive and self-assured approach required of journalists often runs counter to cultural norms for women. Many sources expect journalists to be male, which when coupled with sexist language on assignments (e.g., "Gentlemen of the press ..."), often leaves women feeling like intruders in a man's world. Sexual harassment by both colleagues and information sources, along with salary discrimination, lack of opportunities for training, and lack of role models contribute to the erosion of women's self-esteem and determination to excel. Moreover, the conflict between taxing working conditions and domestic responsibilities often force women to pass up career-boosting essential extras – working long hours, networking with colleagues, strengthening and seeking out new sources, making oneself available to cover breaking news or to travel or for training opportunities that take place outside of the standard nine-to-five working day – which puts them at a disadvantage in competing for the best jobs and assignments (Adagala and Kiai, 1994; Gallagher and von Euler, 1995; Houenassou-Houangbe, 1992; Kamotho, 1990; International Women's Media Foundation Survey, 1995).

It is widely accepted that greater involvement by women in both the technical and decision-making areas of communication and media would improve both the content of media coverage as well as the context in which women journalists work.

Images and Portrayals

Gender-based stereotyping can be found in public and private, local, national and international media organisations – electronic, print, visual and audio. The media is often criticised for perpetuating images that reduce women to sex objects, and for promoting violence against women as 'entertainment'. Degrading images negatively affect women and distort men's attitudes towards women and children by fixing them to their physical attributes and making no recognition of the complex realities of their lives. Programming that reinforces women's traditional roles, particularly in the family, can be equally limiting (Nicholson, 1995; Toronto Declaration, 1995; Global Media Monitoring Project, 1995).

Advertising, in particular, often offers lurid sexual innuendoes aimed at men and which demean women as appendages or reinforce the notion of women as mere objects. All too often these include ads by public sector entities seeking international investments in tourism and manufacturing. In a two-month study of the Asian edition of Newsweek, Ling found the most stereotypical images to be tourist ads that showed smiling Asian women in traditional dress beckoning the foreign traveller to come and enjoy their "service". One resort tantalises potential male customers with the slogan, "Come to the Banyan Tree with your wife and leave with another woman." But Ling notes that even ads that appear less sensationalist, "are infused with a masculinised, westernised authority," citing as an example an ad for a Hong Kong bank in which three men and a woman are gathered around a table. All are Asian but the men wear crisp Western business suits and are clearly engaged in some sort of business transaction, while the woman – dressed as a worker – is holding a vacuum cleaner and peering over one man's shoulder. "The implicit message: she may be just a cleaning-woman but even her interest is piqued by their stimulating business" (Ling, 1996).

Nicholson (1995) notes a 1987 ad luring investors to Jamaica's Free-Trade Zone where the labour force is largely female, which featured the silhouette of a woman's bottom and legs clad in a mini-skirt under the caption, "Your bottom-line is beautiful when you make it in Jamaica," and another some years later focusing again on a female bottom – this time in brief panties and without the legs – with the words, "a brief example of our work." In this latter case, one notes that the negative images were promoted by a government entity – Jamaica National Investment Promotion (JNIP). It is also useful to note that women did something about it. A public protest led by Sistren Theatre Collective, a grassroots popular theatre NGO, led to the withdrawal of the ad, which was widely criticised for selling the image of young working-class women as sex objects.

In the developing countries particularly, there are additional concerns about the overload of foreign programming in which "the ideal woman presented is usually white, leading an American upper class lifestyle, with alien values and appearance" (de Bruin, 1994), and there is on the one hand a "heavy dosage of ... women of foreign origin" and on the other "a total lack of coverage of Kenyan rural women", on Kenya Television Network (Adagali and Kiai, 1994).

In many developing countries, television fare is restricted by budget constraints. Programming imported from the US, often old series in which the way women are portrayed may be outdated even in the country of origin, may dominate peak viewing times. While it is true that local programming is often expensive to produce and may even lack sophistication, joint productions with local private companies, sensitive pre-screening of programmes from developed countries and exchanges with other developing countries, are some ways to improve this situation. National broadcasting entities can also foster partnerships with community groups using video for community development.

Media and Violence in Society

Gender stereotyping by the media leads women, men and children to develop false and stultifying views and expectations of themselves and others, and masks reality. When women and men fail to match up to the fantasy ideal created by the media, serious problems may arise. Both women and men may develop low self-esteem. Women are more likely to become depressed and accepting of abuse, while men are more likely to become frustrated and angry, leading to violent and abusive behaviour.

The high incidence of media violence worldwide – whether verbal, physical, psychological and/or sexual – is of great concern and has generated debate and research into just how media violence affects viewers, in particular children. Media violence is insidious since the viewer may perceive no visible long-term effects. It is appealing since it is so often linked with power, and it is shown as a quick way of resolving conflicts.

How much violence is there on television (for many the most hypnotic of all media)? The US company TV Guide, in a 1995 study based on 18 hours of viewing (6:00 a.m.-12:00 midnight) on 10 channels (ABC, CBS, NBC, FOX, PBS affiliates; plus the cable channels: WTBS, USA Network, MTV, HBO) in Washington DC, concluded that "violence remains a pervasive, major feature of contemporary television programming, and it is coming from more sources and in greater volume than ever before."

The study cited 1,846 individual acts of violence – ranging from violence that resulted in one or more fatalities, to threatening behaviour with a weapon. Cartoons had the most violent scenes (471), followed by promos for TV shows (265), movies (221), toy commercials (188), music videos (123), and commercials for movies (121). Numerous other North American research projects had already ascertained the link between media violence and violence in the society[3] (Nicholson et al, 1997). Media watchdog groups in all continents have proved most effective in raising public awareness of these issues.[4]

Women's Alternative Media Networks

Riano's *Typology of Women's Participation in Communication* (1994) identifies the discourse and practices of four major frameworks: development communication (women as subjects of information); participatory communication (women as participants); alternative communication (women as subjects of change); and feminist communication (women as producers of meaning). Within their organisations and more broadly within civil society, women have used all these types of communication to achieve their development goals.

During the 1960s and 1970s, women's groups in developing countries responded to their negative portrayal in the mainstream media by establishing media monitoring and social action groups. The literature recognises "a growing number of women's information networks, linking researchers, journalists, and activists across countries and regions" (Riano, 1994). Concerned as they are with "the basic needs of their societies ... the creation of life and the preservation of the environment," and recognising that they are "at the bottom of all hierarchies," there are many women communicators, in all continents, who see their role "as one of ensuring that women's interests, aspirations and visions are centrally located and disseminated" (Bangkok Declaration, 1994).

The creation of alternative presses has opened new publishing opportunities for women. Worldwide networks of independent video makers and filmmakers are developing a variety of visual alternatives and narratives (Riano, 1994). In Asia, despite constraints of scale and heterogeneity "several serious attempts have been made" to establish solid women's media networks at both regional and national levels (Balakrishnan, 1994). In the Caribbean, "each country has its own set of women's organisations producing and using alternative media as fora for women's issues" (Francis-Brown et al, 1995). In Africa, women using folk media (oral history, traditional performing arts, etc.) "fulfil a variety of functions from transmitting information to improving thinking ability, to instilling values and shaping a world view, lobbying for social causes and a variety of other educational causes" (Adagala et al, 1994).

Women are now able to move information around the globe even faster than some governments through watchdog networks that combine fax-trees, e-mail, postal services and word of mouth. One such example is that of the global fax and electronic networks-Women's Global Faxnet and Women's GlobalNet, which developed from a fax network, WomeNet, started by 14 women communicators from 10 women's media networks in nine countries at a workshop in Barbados in 1992. A support and solidarity mechanism aimed at exchanging information and alerting each other to national and regional developments affecting women, WomeNet (by then 28 organisations strong) came into its own when women bound for the UN Fourth World Conference on Women in Beijing protested efforts to marginalise them from the proceedings. Once the first fax alert went out from International Women's Tribune Centre (IWTC) in New York, it took just four days for 111 organisations in 40 countries of eight world regions to fax protest letters to the UN Secretary-General. "Within six weeks, the WomeNet had evolved into a Global Faxnet servicing over 500 organisations, groups and individuals, and it had generated an estimated 3,000 signed petitions and protest letters from women's organisations, global networks, NGOs and even governmental bodies, in over 100 countries in every region" (Ross Frankson, 1996).

The Beijing Platform for Action, in recognition of the important role of women's alternative media networks, calls for governments "to support the development of and finance, as appropriate, alternative media and the use of all means of communication to disseminate information to and about women and their concerns" (Paragraph 245e).

Ministries of Information and Communication can link up, support, and benefit from women's alternative media organisations in respect of their outreach, innovative uses of local culture, and their perspectives. A first step is to recognise their work, contribution and expertise by including their representatives in policy-making – on advisory boards, and editorial groups – and as experts in programming. Ministries may also seek to partner with women's alternative media networks for education purposes: in awareness-building workshops for ministry and public service broadcasting personnel, for public sensitisation campaigns, and for media awareness training in schools.

Electronic Communications

The general findings of an Associated Progressive Communications (APC) survey (*Networking for Change*, May 1997)[5] reveal that women are making great strides in adopting electronic communications, and have benefited from the support and facilitation provided by proactive initiatives. Increased communication and sharing of knowledge among women, particularly in the developing South but also in Eastern Europe and remote communities in the North, has broadened the scope of on-line participation creating a more equitable global women's forum on-line. For many women who knew very little about computer communications just a few years ago, using e-mail has become a routine part of their day-to-day lives.

Women in the South – particularly Africa and Asia – and in Eastern Europe, primarily use e-mail, conferencing and listservs, while women in the North show greater use of Internet tools, such as search engines and the World Wide Web. These regional differences are due to access issues, such as infrastructure limitations or costs to connect, rather than lack of interest or motivation on the part of women to adopt the newer technologies.

Of particular note for ministries of information and communications as they seek to raise public awareness about gender issues is the fact that many connected women, particularly in the developing South, act as bridges to unconnected groups in their communities by repackaging information they find on-line and sharing it through other communication channels such as print, fax, telephone, radio, theatre, etc.

The challenges and pitfalls of electronic communications include limited accessibility, information overload, language constraints, skill deficiencies, and lack of gender-sensitive training. Women in the developing South face particular challenges: limitations of e-mail only accounts (not having access to remote databases or Internet tools); limited infrastructure (difficulty in getting a phone line); and the high costs of data transmission (networks in the South often charge their users for all messages, both sent and received).

The APC survey identified lack of training, the high cost of equipment and lack of time and human resources as common barriers and concluded that it was necessary to encourage local expertise in efficient and cost-effective computer networking technologies.

Research

Existing literature on women's portrayal by, access to, and employment in the media is still heavily dominated by research from North America and Western Europe. Studies from other parts of the world, where they do exist, are often limited in their scope. "Very few studies have been done regarding gender and media audiences in Africa" (Adagala and Kiai, 1994). "There is no systematic documentation on the position of women in Caribbean media, their influence or lack of influence, their power or lack of power" (de Bruin, 1995). In Asia "there are very scant studies on media's position vis-à-vis socio-political and economic structures and the concomitant effects on women" (Balakrishnan, 1994).

Apart from the need to develop and strengthen data bases about women and media, research should be used as the basis for action that productively enhances women's relationship to the media. The research should also be used to develop appropriate support materials. With regard to electronic communications, for instance, computer manuals, 'how-to' books, instructional guides and access resources tend to be written for North American and other Western audiences: they are expensive, full of technical jargon and assume an infrastructure and knowledge base that may not exist in less-developed contexts. Moreover, they rarely contain either gender- or culturally-sensitive wording or examples. Materials written in local languages that simplify the technical jargon, contain recognisable images, and are geared towards community realities would be a welcome first step for increasing women's interest in electronic communications.

Training

In all regions the number of women in higher education journalism courses has been increasing. White (1992) found that at the University of Nairobi School of Journalism, "the number and proportion of women students (had) steadily increased until 1991 when there were actually more women than men in the ... postgraduate training programmes." Balakrishnan (1994) says that "in all parts of Asia, women outnumber men in at least some of the programmes," and in Southeast Asia and Australia "women outnumber men in all communications programmes." UNESCO figures show that women now account for 52 per cent of all students in journalism and mass communication schools in Europe, but women who enter journalism education are "more likely than men to quit the profession through frustration or disillusionment" (van Zoonan, 1989). At the same time, few courses are tailored specifically for gender concerns even where courses in development communications exist. In Kenya, despite a strong presence of women in formal training programmes, Kibutiri (1990) found that 56 per cent of media women "did not feel adequately trained to tackle gender issues."

Women-specific training that is free is recommended particularly in the area of electronic communications. Studies have recorded different tendencies between women and men in their ease and use of electronic communications; for example, men tend to start with hands-on exploration, while women first want to know how it all works. Women have less access to electronic communications and less ownership of equipment. They therefore tend to be less proactive in learning the new technologies and need more initial encouragement and training. The main difference is not related to capacity to learn or even eagerness, but in approach: many women are more comfortable learning in women-only or women-centred environments (APC Survey, 1997).

Notes

1   As noted by Gallagher (1994), the Australian born Murdoch also controls – *inter alia* – 60% of the Australian press, 40% of the UK press, the entire press of Fiji, a US TV network, a Hollywood studio, the largest circulation magazine in the US and a major international book publisher (*TV World Guide to Asia*, October 1993).

2   Co-ordinated and facilitated by Women's MediaWatch, Canada, this study is based on 49,000 data records collected by groups and individuals in 71 countries on the same day, January 18, 1995. The monitoring project gave women a tool with which to scrutinise media output and document the gender bias that exists in news content worldwide. Taking part were teachers and academics, activists and lobbyists, journalists and other media professionals, some with research experience, others with none. In some countries, disparate groups co-operated for the first time, united by their concern about the portrayal of women by their national media.

3   Among them: the National Commission on the Causes and Prevention of Violence (1968); the Surgeon General's Report (1972); the National Institute for Mental Health's study on Media Images and Violence (1982); and the US Attorney General's Task Force on Family Violence (1984).

4   Ten years ago when Women's Media Watch Jamaica (WMWJ) was formed to "clean up the negative images of women in the Jamaican media, and raise public awareness around the issues," it was seen as "too feminist, too middle-class and totally impractical," but nowadays "the radio talk shows seem full of women and men complaining about an ad or programme they find offensive." In the period WMWJ has conducted hundreds of workshops in Jamaica and overseas, designed and conducted scores of public campaigns, lobbied the media and government bodies, helped establish similar groups in Trinidad and Tobago and Barbados, and works closely with the Jamaica Broadcasting Commission and is represented on Inter-Press Service's editorial committee and the National Cinematographic Authority, according to Melody Walker in Ms magazine (Jan/Feb 1998).

5   Aimed at identifying women's electronic networking needs and opportunities around the world, the survey findings are based on 147 responses from a diversity of groups and individuals in 36 countries. The survey was e-mailed to over 700 women's groups and individuals working on issues of concern to women in both the public and the private sectors.

4 Strategies and Recommendations for Action

The following are strategic areas in which action can be taken to advance gender equality in the information and communications sector:

+ the policy environment;
+ image and portrayal of women and men;
+ employment, production and programming;
+ outreach and democratisation;
+ training;
+ research; and
+ gender-sensitive action tools.

In each of these strategic areas, a number of recommendations for action are suggested. Governments may wish to adapt these recommendations to suit their particular national circumstances and priorities. In addition, some specific tools are provided in this manual for use in carrying out the recommended actions.

Since in most countries the media are overwhelmingly male-controlled and portray women largely in terms of limited stereotypes, the strategies recommended here focus mainly on closing the gender gap for women. In countries where male marginalisation is an emerging problem, attention should be paid to the role of the media in reversing this trend. There is also a need to focus on the role of the media in re-socialising both women and men, and changing traditional attitudes, behaviours and roles that perpetuate gender stereotypes and inequalities.

The policy environment

+ Review existing policies – legislation, guidelines, codes of ethics – with a view to integrating a gender perspective aimed at enhancing women's skills, knowledge, access, and participation in all types of media, including on-line technologies (see Figure 2 and Appendix 1).
+ Encourage the creation and/or strengthening of professional guidelines and codes of conduct or other self-regulatory mechanisms for the media with a view to eliminating gender-biased programming.
+ Ensure gender balance in all government, parliamentary, state or public entities that consider media, advertising and telecommunications policy.
+ Enact appropriate legislation against pornography and the projection of violence against women and children in the media.
+ Abolish laws which effectively curb freedom of expression and/or freedom of association, and that result in discrimination against women.

Image and portrayal of women and men

+ Promote balanced and diverse media portrayals of women as persons who bring to their positions many different life experiences – as politicians, peace negotiators,

Figure 2	Tool for Gender Analysis

This tool provides general guidelines for formulating and assessing gender in projects, training, and programming.

Basic questions to ask about how any particular activity, decision or plan will affect women and men.

1 **Who does what?** Analysing the division of labour between women and men in the system being analysed.

2 **Who has what?** Access to property, entitlements and decision rights over private and public resources in the system.

3 **What factors influence this gender arrangement?** Identify factors – culture, law, economics and political policy – that influence this gender arrangement, how they are changing if at all, and what needs to be done to promote change.

4 **How are public and private sector resources distributed and who gets what?** Which institutional structures are used, their degree of equity and efficiency, and how to make these more responsive to women and men.

5 **Are planners listening to women?** Don't ignore, discount or minimise their information and observations as 'women's complaints'.

6 **Are spaces being created for women to identify and articulate their own needs, strategies and solutions?**

7 **Is it recognised that women's lives encompass a variety of productive and reproductive activities which are often discounted in sectoral planning?**

8 **Is gender-based violence against women being taken into consideration in programme and policy design?** Prevention mechanisms against coercion and abuse of power should be incorporated into development initiatives.

9 **Is women's productive work being made visible?** Employ sex-differentiated data and comparative analysis to identify and measure women's contributions.

10 **Is analysis of gender relations being extended beyond the circle of kin and community to include such spheres as legislative bodies, international institutions and the global market?** Address the process of transforming gender relations at all levels: household, community, regional, national and international.

11 **Are personal gender biases being examined and internalised assumptions about women's and men's roles being challenged?**

professionals, managers, entrepreneurs and mothers – to provide role models for young women.

✦ Provide positive role-models for young males and avoid reinforcing stereotypical images of masculinity and femininity that perpetuate gender inequalities.

✦ Promote the use of non-sexist, gender-sensitive language (see Figure 3).

✦ Exclude stereotyped images, and violent and/or pornographic materials that discriminate against or that violate women's and children's rights in information, advertisements, marketing, and entertainment (see Figure 4).

✦ Increase the number of programmes for, by and about women.

✦ Increase women's participation, particularly in the portrayal of traditionally male-dominated areas of society linked to power and influence (e.g., politics, peace negotiations, economics, business).

✦ Broaden sources – women, youth, indigenous people can speak on any issue and on all aspects of life.

✦ Create and/or strengthen broad-based media monitoring entities and encourage easy access procedures for adequate consideration of consumer complaints lodged with media enterprises or advertisers against media content or advertisements that portray women or men in a discriminatory way.

Employment

+ Ensure equal employment opportunities for women at all levels of the media industry – management, production and programming, design, administration, technical, and education and training.
+ Adopt positive action programmes, including equal pay for equal work, equal access to training, fair and transparent promotion procedures, targets and timetables to achieve a fair proportion of women in decision-making positions, and action against sexual harassment, so that women can reach their full potential as media professionals.
+ Create opportunities to increase women's ownership of media houses and directorship of media organisations.
+ Attract and retain women in the profession by devising family friendly support facilities aimed at easing the conflict women journalists face between taxing and unpredictable working conditions and family responsibilities. These could include job sharing and flexitime, easy access child care, parental leave, re-entry support, and telecommuting.

Production and programming

+ Apply gender analysis to programming and develop editorial policies that are gender-sensitive and reflect gender equity, so that women's and men's perspectives are equally included in all topics.
+ Provide incentives for creative, gender-sensitive programming in the national media.
+ Disseminate information on development and social issues in local languages, using traditional, indigenous and other forms of media, such as story telling, drama, poetry and song.
+ Devise media campaigns that promote gender equality, such as equal sharing of family responsibilities, and provide information aimed at eliminating domestic violence and all other forms of violence against women and children.
+ Target gender-awareness programmes at both women and men.
+ Sensitise media managers and professionals to increase coverage of women's points of view, especially in political, economic, business and scientific news.
+ Recognise women as authoritative information sources, experts, and opinion makers – and therefore news sources on any issue, and not confine women to the role of speaking only on 'women's issues.'
+ Introduce, support and extend community radio stations as a way of increasing women's participation and contribution to the media and local economic development, especially in areas of high illiteracy rates.

Outreach and democratisation

+ Develop and support monitoring bodies and media watch groups that survey media and advertising content concerning gender portrayal.
+ Include media women in media self-regulatory committees and other executive committees that draft programme guidelines, budgets, contracts and personnel documents.
+ Support local, regional, national and international networks for women media professionals and promote active North/South and South/South co-operation between journalists' organisations, women's professional media associations, women's legal groups and women's political associations.

Figure 3	Guidelines For Gender-Sensitive Language

These guidelines provide alternatives to ambiguous and stereotypical words and phrases and traditional titles and forms of address. They can be used to build gender-awareness and sensitivity among ministry and media personnel.

Traditional	Alternative
Mr and Mrs John Smith	Jane and John Smith; Mr and Mrs Smith; Mr and Ms Smith
Miss, Mrs	Ms (female equivalent to Mr - does not indicate marital status, which is often irrelevant)
Chairman	Chair; Chairperson (Chairwoman or Chairman for specific cases)
girl	woman; young woman; girl-child
men and girls	girls and boys/boys and girls; women and men/men and women
man and wife	husband and wife; wife and husband
housewife	homemaker
lady	woman (unless the parallel is to 'gentleman')
emasculated	weakened; enfeebled; diminished; toothless; tame; watered-down
effeminate	delicate; feeble; fussy; soft; languid; affected; gentle
forefathers	forebears; ancestors
founding fathers	founders
authoress; poetess; actress	author; poet; actor
women's lib	women's movement
women's libber	feminist; supporter of the women's movement
businessman	business manager; executive; agent; representative (plural: business people; business community)
cameraman	photographer; camera operator (plural: camera crew)
foreman	supervisor
policeman/men	police officer (plural: police)
craftsman	artisan; craftworker
statesman	political leaders, statesman or woman
statesmanship	statescraft
spokesman	spokesperson; spokesman or woman (for specific person)
man-made	artificial; synthetic; manufactured; industrial
manpower	staff; labour; workforce; personnel; workers; human resources
salesman/girl	assistant; attendant (plural: salespersons)
steward/stewardess	staff; crew
man, mankind	people, humanity; human beings; the human race; men and women; homo sapiens; the public; society
brotherhood of man	human fellowship; human kinship; solidarity
primitive man	primitive people or peoples; primitive women and men
man a project	staff a project; hire personnel; employ staff
mother tongue	first language
committee of wise men	committee of counsellors; eminent persons; advisory panel

Adjective bias

a) ambitious/aggressive/outspoken/strident; b) cautious/timid/emotional/ hysterical – these words may apply to men, women, people or individuals but when either set is applied selectively to men (a) and women (b) they connote bias.

Pronouns

The pronoun 'his' when used in general situations – e.g., 'Anyone disagreeing with the statement should give his reasons' – should be pluralised (their) or used to a limited extent as 'his' or 'her' only when it applies to all. S/he may also be used where appropriate.

Roles

Avoid stereotyped assumptions about the roles of men and women. For example, the sentence, 'Research scientists often neglect their wives and children,' assumes that women are not research scientists, whereas a simple change – 'Research scientists often neglect their families,' acknowledges that women as well as men are research scientists; similarly, 'Transport will be provided for delegates and their wives,' assumes all delegates are men whereas, 'Transport will be provided for delegates and their spouses,' correctly recognises women as well as men in the role of delegate.

Source: "Fair Exposure Guidelines for the Constructive and Positive Portrayal and Presentation of Women in the Media", Status of Women Office, Australia, 1993.

Figure 4	Fair Exposure Guidelines

This tool provides suggestions for developing guidelines for the constructive and positive portrayal and presentation of women in the media:

✦ specific in nature but general enough to avoid the label of censorship (e.g. broadcasters, publishers, advertisers and media practitioners are encouraged 'to write, illustrate, edit and present with a sense of equality, appropriateness and dignity for both sexes.')

✦ alternatives to commonly used sexist language (e.g. 'homemaker' or 'houseworker' instead of 'housewife'; 'police officer' to replace 'policeman')

✦ checklist to help advertisers eliminate offensive advertising (e.g., Do your advertisements portray women as sex objects or contain double entendre particularly about sex or women's bodies? Do the ads portray women in situations which are potentially sexually dangerous, or as victims of violence?)

✦ contact list of people who should be addressed for complaints (plus a recommendation that copies be sent to the offending publication, advertisers or broadcast station)

✦ Develop and/or increase linkages with women's media networks including electronic networks and other new technologies of communication, and assist the financing of these networks.

✦ Advise smaller media, especially those reaching women in rural and marginalised urban areas, on questions such as available technology optimal for their needs.

✦ Interlink more effectively grassroots workers and volunteers, media researchers, NGOs, advocacy groups, alternative media networks and policy-makers concerning women and the media.

✦ Create networks among, and develop information-exchange programmes between NGOs, women's organisations and professional media organisations with a view to increasing women's participation in media.

✦ Promote media literacy programmes for the public at large in order to develop the critical faculties needed for analysing messages disseminated by the media, and to prevent prejudice that may be caused by television's depiction of violence against women. Conduct these programmes through national education curricula and in informal education activities at community level with women and men, young and old.

✦ Encourage dialogue between the media sector and the field of education in general to raise public awareness of the portrayal of women in the media.

✦ Partner public and private educational institutions to disseminate information about, and increase awareness of, women's human rights, particularly in respect of all forms of violence against women.

✦ Work in co-operation with journalists' organisations to develop guidelines against gender-biased treatment of information, and checklists against gender-biased language for reporters and editors to use when writing and reviewing stories.

✦ Promote dialogue between organisations of journalists and media employers to discuss a joint approach to the ethics of gender portrayal.

Training

✦ Assign programme budgets to allow for women's and men's equal access to all forms of professional training.

✦ Include training modules in gender-awareness, local history and cultural diversity at all media training institutions.

✦ Train women media students and professionals in management and related subjects, such as interpersonal communication and decision-making skills, with a view to promoting women's media enterprises.

✦ Develop train-the-trainer programmes geared specifically for women in computing and all new communications technologies.

✦ Develop educational and training methodologies that enable women's organisations and community groups to effectively communicate their own messages and concerns and access to existing media.

✦ Encourage gender-sensitive training for media professionals including media owners and managers, to encourage the creation and use of non-stereotyped, balanced and diverse images of women and men in the media.

✦ Sponsor short-term or longer term professional internships or exchanges to expand the professional skills of women media professionals.

Research

✦ Increase research into all aspects of women and media – including alternative, traditional, local, and folk forms, as well as new communications technologies used by women – to define areas needing attention and action.

✦ Undertake national studies on media audiences and the impact on viewers of the content of media products, especially in respect of violence against women. Include the development of follow-up and evaluation systems.

✦ Ensure all national statistics are disaggregated by sex, to facilitate national analysis and planning in the gender mainstreaming process. Aim to repackage research for wide dissemination.

Gender-sensitive action tools

✦ Build and make widely available a data base on women working in the media in all fields (see Figure 5).

✦ Publish pertinent studies – for example on women's portrayal by the media, women's employment in the media, listening, viewing and reading patterns, media policies and patterns of media ownership – that can assist in building the base for gender-aware evaluation and planning.

◆ Collect and distribute annual bibliographies on major research activities and findings concerning women in communication and development.

◆ Create a data base of resource materials produced by national women's machineries and women's alternative media networks at local, national, regional and international levels.

◆ Repackage legislation and international conventions on women in simplified forms and in local languages for wide dissemination.

◆ Facilitate the compilation of a Directory of Women Media Experts.

◆ Develop, and maintain with regular updates, a Media Directory of women spokespersons for use by journalists and media practitioners.

◆ Set up an international on-line network for exchange of information on portrayal of women in the media and information on women's media enterprises.

◆ Disseminate non-sexist language guidelines.

◆ Establish, in co-operation with broadcasters, an international video library on women for use in programming but also to be used in seminars and workshops aimed at raising awareness of media professionals and the general public.

◆ Circulate regular information sheets on funders interested in the development of communication projects relating to women, alternative media networks, independent women media professionals and NGOs working in popular media forms.

◆ Facilitate the distribution and marketing efforts of women's independent presses and newsletters focusing on women, gender relations and development.

Figure 5   **Women Journalists'/Media Workers' Questionnaire**

This questionnaire can be used to build a database on women working in media.

1 Do you, as a woman journalist, find yourself or your female colleagues facing obstacles that your male counterparts do not face?   Yes ■ No ■

2 If so, what are some of these obstacles?
Lack of educational opportunities ■
Lack of access to information ■
Denial of equal pay for equal work ■
Denial of access to assignments ■
Lack of role models ■
Balancing family/work ■
Sexual harassment ■
Other (specify)

None ■

3 Are these obstacles generally considered to be a problem among women in your organisation?   Yes ■ No ■ Don't know ■

4 In general, do your male colleagues believe that such problems faced by women are a problem for the company and/or the media industry?   Yes ■ No ■ Don't know ■

5 In general, is the salary scale different for men and women journalists working at the same level?   Yes ■ No ■ Don't know ■

6 Which of the following initiatives/mechanisms would you like to see strengthened or put in place to help remove the barriers that women face as media professionals:
Legislative/legal ■
Women's media associations/organisations ■
Women's divisions in journalism associations ■
Educational ■
Other (specify)

None ■

7 What is your view of how women are portrayed in the media?
The media generally portrays women accurately.   Yes ■ No ■ Sometimes ■
The media generally misrepresents women.   Yes ■ No ■ Sometimes ■
The media often disregards women as leaders.   Yes ■ No ■ Sometimes ■

8 Is there a women's journalism organisation available to you?   Yes ■ No ■

5 Models of Good Practice

Action Model 1: Mainstreaming Gender in Editorial Policy and Practice

The implementation plan adopted by the Caribbean office of the Inter-press Service (IPS) Third World News Agency for mainstreaming gender in editorial policy and output has the following implementation structure:

The editorial committee

What is it? The primary support system for gender-aware mainstreaming policies and activities.

Who is on it? It comprises some 20-30 persons that together reflect a diverse representation of Caribbean society. They are currently based primarily in Kingston, Jamaica, where IPS Caribbean is located. The aim is to continue expanding the pool of contributors to include members from the wider Caribbean.

How are committee members selected? Members of the Editorial Committee were identified in consultation with regional gender and media experts and researchers.

What do they contribute to the process? The members meet on a rotational basis each month with the Gender Co-ordinator and a Gender Consultant. They provide ideas, angles and new sources for the monthly editorial story agenda. They select stories within the framework of the commitments made to women in the United Nations Fourth World Conference on Women Platform for Action. Committee members are expected to be proactive in identifying and alerting the Gender Co-ordinator to studies and other sources of information, including data bases and information available on the world wide web that can strengthen IPS Caribbean's access to gender-aware information. The Committee also provides ideas and offers collaboration in the development of training and other activities for implementing the policy goals, for example opening collaboration between IPS Caribbean and women's groups and NGOs aimed at improving their capacity to use the media and increasing the presence of their voices in the news.

What resources are available? A limited supplemental budget is available to fund the stories identified in the monthly meetings, where necessary.

The Gender Editorial Committee Co-ordinator

The Gender Co-ordinator, who is also the Regional Editor, is responsible on a day-to-day basis for the monitoring and implementation of goals, policies and activities of the overall policy. S/he is also responsible for inter-regional communications and sharing of experiences and information among regional gender teams or committees. S/he convenes meetings of the editorial committee and oversees committee inputs from proposal through planning and implementation. Employs and oversees part-time administrative support required for operation of the committee process.

The Gender, Media and Development Consultant

The Gender, Media and Development Consultant is an expert who provides technical support to the Gender Co-ordinator. S/he is expected to help develop the Gender Co-ordinator's expertise by transferring skills and knowledge, providing implementing tools, and contributing to monitoring and evaluation tasks to ensure effective results in the initial stages of the implementation plan. Specifically, in support of the Regional Editor/Gender Co-ordinator, the consultant will read and assess the daily cast, and provide a fortnightly analysis and feedback notes for use in discussions with reporters and stringers.

Steps in establishing the process

Phase one: Recruit a gender consultant and part time administrative support staff. Conduct a baseline content analysis of regional copy. Obtain content analysis studies and other major relevant papers on the portrayal of women in media. Compile information on possible funding sources for project activities. Contact women and gender experts (target universities, alternative women's media networks, the national machineries for the advancement of women, professional media organisations), and compile a list of possible persons to serve on the editorial committee.

Phase two: Issue invitations detailing the project's purpose to potential editorial committee members. Hold first meeting and begin feeding story ideas into the monthly editorial agenda. Together with senior reporters, draft explanatory background information and distribution of the policy, guidelines, format requirements and checklists for initial implementation. Begin monitoring implementation of the monthly editorial story agenda.

Phase three: Integrate remaining reporting staff into the implementation process. Report the results of the baseline regional content analysis to all the actors. Hold a second meeting of the editorial committee aimed at setting a second monthly editorial story agenda, organising project proposals development ideas and assigning resources.

Phase four: Produce project proposals for retreats/workshops that bring together all editorial staff with committee members and other interested parties. Conduct evaluation and progress assessments. Devise a one-year-workplan and submit funding requirements.

Action Model 2: Creating a Gender Programme for Working Journalists

The Caribbean Institute for Mass Communications (CARIMAC) gender programme includes the following components:

Course module: A 13-week course module on Media, Gender and Development was designed for use in a regular university setting.

Training travel kit: The above module was adapted into a 'travel kit' for use in short-term workshops for practising journalists across the Caribbean region.

Publication: CARIMAC published a Caribbean resource book for journalists, *Women and Caribbean Media*. It is the first study to provide baseline information on trends within media organisations, both mainstream and alternative in the Caribbean region.

Follow-up research: A study on women's employment patterns in Caribbean media aimed at extending the research findings of the above publication, specifically in respect of detailing the extent of women's concentration in the lower echelons. Among the many questions raised were: How do women move into decision-making positions and how do men respond to their upward mobility? What are the psychological barriers that women in high positions face? Why are more women found in management positions in the electronic media as opposed to the print media? To what extent does the presence of women make a difference to output? What is the career path of female CARIMAC graduates and how does it differ from that of male graduates? Comparatively how many women and men leave media organisations in mid-career and why?

Outreach: The training course and 'travel kit' were designed and developed in collaboration with a wide range of actors: Caribbean Community (CARICOM) Women's Desk; Caribbean Office of the UN Development Fund for Women (UNIFEM); the University of the West Indies' Centre for Gender and Development Studies (CGDS), and Women and Development Unit (WAND); Caribbean News Agency (CANA); and CARIMAC. The publication includes contributions by a broad grouping of women in different fields of media expertise – alternative media, academia, government information policy. The collaborative research made use of CARIMAC's extended network of graduates across the region.

References

Abu Nasr, J and Abul-Husn, R (1994). "Among Veils and Walls: Women and Media in the Middle East," in *Women Empowering Communication: A Resource Book on Women and the Globalisation of Media*. London: WAAC; Manila: Isis International; New York: IWTC.

Adagala, E and Kiai, W (1994). "Folk, Interpersonal and Mass Media – The Experience of Women in Africa," in *Women Empowering Communication: A Resource Book on Women and the Globalisation of Media*. London: WAAC; Manila: Isis International; New York: IWTC.

Allen, D (1994). "Women in Media, Women's Media: The Search for Linkages in North America," in *Women Empowering Communication: A Resource Book on Women and the Globalisation of Media*. London: WAAC; Manila: Isis International; New York: IWTC.

Anand, A (1994). "Starting Up, Staying There and Moving On," Paper presented to the WACC/ISIS/IWTC Women Empowering Communications Conference. Bangkok, Thailand.

Association for Progressive Communications (APC) (May 1997). Women's Networking Support Programme Survey. *Global Networking for Change: Experiences from the APC Women's Programme*.

Balakrishnan, V (1994). "Indigenous Social Norms and Women in Asian Media," in *Women Empowering Communication: A Resource Book on Women and the Globalisation of Media*. London: WAAC; Manila: Isis International; New York: IWTC.

The Bangkok Declaration: Women Empowering Communication Conference (February 1994). World Association for Christian Communication (WACC)/Isis Manila/International Women's Tribune Centre (IWTC).

Barriteau-Foster, E (1992). "The Construct of a Post-Modernist Feminist Theory for Caribbean Social Science," *Social and Economic Research*, Vol. 41, No 2. University of the West Indies.

Bonder, G and Zurutuza, C (1993). "Mujer y Comunicacion en Argentina." Unpublished Report. Santo Domingo, Dominican Republic: United Nations International Research and Training Institute for the Advancement of Women (INSTRAW).

Brown, M E (1990). *Television and Women's Culture: The Politics of the Popular*. London/Newbury Park/New Delhi: Sage Publications.

Commonwealth Secretariat (1999). Gender Management System Handbook. Gender Management System Series. London: Commonwealth Secretariat.

De Bruin, M (1995). "Gender and the Context of Media Work," in *Media, Gender and Development: A Resource Book for Journalists*. Jamaica: CARIMAC.

Eisler, R (1996). "Communication, Socialisation and Domination: The Replication of Violence and the Partnership Alternative," in *Women Transforming Communications: Global Connections*.

Farr, E and Chitiga, R (1991). *Hello, Is Gender There? A Study of Gender Awareness in the MS Programme in Zimbabwe*.

Francis-Brown, S (ed.) (1995). *Media, Gender and Development: A Resource Book for Journalists*. Jamaica: CARIMAC.

Gallagher, M (ed.) (1994). *Women Empowering Media: A Resource Book on Women and the Globalisation of Media*. London: WAAC; Manila: Isis International; New York: IWTC

Gallagher, M and von Euler, M (1996). *Women's Participation in the News- Africa, Caribbean and Central America, Pacific, Asia*. London: WAAC.

Gallagher, M and von Euler, M (1995). *An Unfinished Story: Gender Patterns in Media Employment*. Reports and Papers on Mass Communication. UNESCO Publishing.

Global Media Monitoring Project (1995). *Women's Participation in the News. National Watch on Images of Women in the Media*. Toronto, Canada: MediaWatch.

Hosken, F P (1996). "Women and International Communication, the Story of WIN NEWS," in *Women Transforming Communications: Global Intersections*, Allen, D et al. (eds.). Sage Publications.

Houenassou-Houangbe, K D (1992). "Les Femmes des Services de la Communication au Togo," in *Women and the Mass Media in Africa*, Occasional Paper Series #6; Dakar, Senegal: Association of African Women for Research and Development (AWORD).

International Women's Media Foundation Survey (1995). *Women in the Media: Facing Obstacles, Changing Attitudes*.

Jackins, H et al (January 1999). "The Human Male: A Men's Liberation Draft Policy," in *Present Time*, no. 114 (vol.31, No.1).

Kabeer, N (1990). "Gender, Development and Training: Raising Awareness in Development Planning". Paper presented to the National Labour Institute/Ford Foundation Workshop on Gender Training and Development. Bangalore, India, November 29-December 6, 1990.

Kabeer, N (1996). "Gender-Aware Policy and Planning: A Social Relations Perspective. Report on the Indo-British Work on Analytical Gender Relations Framework for Development Planning and Practice" : 21-36. Punjab University, India: Centre for Women's Studies and Development.

Kamotho, K (1990). "How Women Journalists in Kenya Perceive Their Role". Research Thesis. School of Journalism, University of Nairobi.

Kibutiri, L (1990). "The Role of Media Women Practitioners in Promoting the Status of Women in Kenya," as quoted by Adagala, E and Kiai, W in "Folk, Interpersonal and Mass Media: The Experience of Women in Africa," in Gallagher, M and Quindoza-Santiago, L (eds.) (1994). *Women Empowering Communication*. London: WACC; Manilla: Isis; New York: IWTC.

Leo-Rhynie, E (1995). "Defining and Discussing Gender: A Caribbean Perspective," in *Media, Gender and Development: A Resource Book for Journalists*. Francis-Brown, S (ed.). Jamaica: Caribbean Institute for Mass Communications (CARIMAC).

Ling, L (1996). "Feminist International Relations: From Critique to Reconstruction". *The Journal of International Communication* (JIC) vol.31, No.1.

Lull, J (ed.) (1988). *World Families Watch Television*. London: Sage Publications.

Moser, C O (1993). *Gender Planning and Development: Theory, Practice and Training*. London and New York: Routledge.

Mytton, G (ed.) (1993). *Global Audiences: Research for Worldwide Broadcasting 1993*. London: John Libbey.

Nicholson, H (1995). "Gender as a Dynamic Concept in the Media," in *Media, Gender and Development: A Resource Book for Journalists*. Francis-Brown, S (ed.). Jamaica: CARIMAC.

Nicholson, H et al. (forthcoming). "Whose Perspective? A Guide to Gender-Sensitive Media Analysis," in *Women's Media Watch Gender Training Manual*.

National Federation of Press Women USA (1993). "NFPW Survey Shows Steady Improvement".

Razavi, S and Miller, C (1995). *Gender Mainstreaming: A Study of Efforts by the UNDP, the World Bank and the ILO to Institutionalise Gender Issues*. Geneva and New York: UNRISD/UNDP.

Riano, P (1994). "Gender in Communication: Women's Contributions," in Pilar Riano (ed.) *Women in Grassroots Communication*. USA/UK/India: Sage Publications.

Ross Frankson, J (1996). "Women's Global FaxNet Charting the Way," in *The Journal of International Communication*. International Association for Media and Communication Research.

Seiter, E; Borchers, H; Kreutzner, G; Warth, E (eds.) (1989). *Remote Control: Audiences and Cultural Power*. London and New York: Routledge.

Sepstrup, P and Goonasekera, A (1994). *TV-Transnationalisation: Europe and Asia*. Reports and papers on Mass Communication #109. London: UNESCO Publishing.

Shallat, L and Paredes, U (1995). *Gender Concepts in Development Planning*. Santo Domingo, Dominican Republic: INSTRAW United Nations International Research and Training Institute for the Advancement of Women.

Sreberny-Mohammadi, A (1994). "Women Talking Politics: Media Realities and Ordinary Lives," in *Perspectives of Women in Television*. London Broadcasting Standards Council Research, Working Paper IX.

Steeves, L H (1990). *Women, Rural Information Delivery and Development in Sub-Saharan Africa*. Working Paper #212, Women in International Development, Michigan State University.

Toronto Platform For Action, UNESCO (1995). "International Symposium on Women and the Media: Access to Expression and Decision-Making", Final Declaration.

United Nations (1996).*The Beijing Declaration and the Platform For Action*, United Nations Fourth World Conference on Women (1995), Beijing, China. New York: United Nations.

Van Zoonen, L (1989). "Professional Socialisation of Feminist Journalists in the Netherlands," in *Women's Studies in Communications*, Vol. 12, No. 2.

Wallace, E (1994). "Media Legislation, Regulation and Policy (On Employment of Women, Portrayal of Women; Treatment of Women's Issues)," in Women in the English-Speaking Caribbean in Gallagher, M. and Quindoza-Santiago, L (eds.), *Women Empowering Communication*. WACC, London/Isis, Manila/IWTC, New York.

Williams, S et al. (1994). *The Oxfam Gender Training Manual*. London: Oxfam.

Appendix 1   *Gender impact assessment questionnaire*

Information and Communications Sector

Groups and individuals may use this questionnaire for assessing the impact of gender on the policy, institutional and media environments, and for planning future action in the process of mainstreaming gender in the agencies, departments and production units of Ministries of Information and Communications.

Assessor Profile

Group

a)   No. of males: .... No. of females: ....

b)   Agency/Department/Team:

_____

_____

_____

c)   Positions within the Agency/Department/Team:

Policymaker	No. of males:	No. of females: ....
Manager	No. of males:	No. of females: ....
Editorial	No. of males:	No. of females: ....
Design	No. of males:	No. of females: ....
Technical	No. of males:	No. off emales: ....
Administration	No. of males:	No. of females: ....
Service	No. of males:	No. of females: ....

Individual

[check box]

a)   male: ☐   female: ☐

b)   Agency/Department/Team:

_____

_____

c) Position within the Agency/Department/Team:

Policymaker   No. of males: ....   No. of females: ....

Manager   No. of males: ....   No. of females: ....

Editorial   No. of males: ....   No. of females: ....

Design   No. of males: ....   No. of females: ....

Technical   No. of males: ....   No. of females: ....

Administration   No. of males: ....   No. of females: ....

Service   No. of males: ....   No. of females: ....

Policy Environment

Existing regulations governing media

a Is there legislation governing the operations of the mass media? [check box]

(i) Radio ☐

(ii) Television ☐

(iii) Film ☐

(iv) Audio ☐

(v) Print ☐

b) Do the regulations make statements regarding [check box]:

(i) the employment of women (equal opportunities)? Yes ☐ No ☐

(ii) the portrayal of women (gender stereotyping)? Yes ☐ No ☐

c) How clear and effective are the statements? [check box]

(i) The employment of women:

very clear ☐   clear ☐   unclear ☐

very effective ☐   effective ☐   ineffective ☐

(ii) The portrayal of women:

very clear ☐   clear ☐   unclear ☐

very effective ☐   effective ☐   ineffective ☐

d) To what extent are these regulations being implemented? [check box]

(i) The employment of women

to a great extent ☐   somewhat ☐   not at all ☐

(ii) The portrayal of women

to a great extent ☐   somewhat ☐   not at all ☐

Nature of existing legislation impacting the media

a) Which of the following laws are in place? [check box]

(i) Libel laws ☐

(ii) Labour laws:
equal pay for equal work ☐
equal opportunities ☐
sexual harassment ☐

(iii) Laws governing the import/distribution of pornography ☐

b) How clear and effective are these laws? [check box]

(i) Libel laws:

very clear ☐   clear ☐   unclear ☐

very effective ☐   effective ☐   ineffective ☐

(ii) Labour laws:

equal pay for equal work

very clear ☐   clear ☐   unclear ☐

very effective ☐   effective ☐   ineffective ☐

equal opportunities

very clear ☐   clear ☐   unclear ☐

very effective ☐   effective ☐   ineffective ☐

sexual harassment

very clear ☐   clear ☐   unclear ☐

very effective ☐   effective ☐   ineffective ☐

(iii) Laws governing the import/distribution of pornography:

very clear ☐   clear ☐   unclear ☐

very effective ☐   effective ☐   ineffective ☐

c) To what extent are these laws being implemented? [check box]

(i) Libel laws:

to a great extent ☐   somewhat ☐   not at all ☐

(ii) Labour laws:

equal pay for equal work

to a great extent ☐   somewhat ☐   not at all ☐

equal opportunities

to a great extent ☐   somewhat ☐   not at all ☐

sexual harassment

to a great extent ☐   somewhat ☐   not at all ☐

(iii) Laws governing the import/distribution of pornography:

to a great extent ☐   somewhat ☐   not at all ☐

Codes/guidelines of conduct governing the portrayal of women in the media

a) Are there existing codes/guidelines of conduct governing the portrayal of women in the media? [check box] Yes ☐ No ☐

b) How clear and effective are these codes/guidelines? [check box]

very clear ☐   clear ☐   unclear ☐

very effective ☐   effective ☐   ineffective ☐

c) To what extent are these codes/guidelines being implemented? [check box]

to a great extent ☐   somewhat ☐   not at all ☐

d) Is there a process for reviewing/upgrading these guidelines/codes? [check box]

Yes ☐ No ☐

e) If Yes, is the review/upgrading process clear and effective? [check box]

very clear ☐   clear ☐   unclear ☐

very effective ☐   effective ☐   ineffective ☐

To what extent are women represented in broadcasting authorities, commissions, and other bodies regulating the media?

a) Name of regulatory body:

_____

No. of males: ....   No. of females: ....

b) Name of regulatory body:

_____

No. of males: ....   No. of females: ....

c) Name of regulatory body:

_____

No. of males: ....   No. of females: ....

d) Name of regulatory body:

_____

No. of males: ....   No. of females: ....

To what extent are the views of the general public sought in formulating policy? [check box]

to a great extent ☐   somewhat ☐   not at all ☐

a)   What instruments are used to obtain the views of the public? [check box]

(i) Opinion polls   ☐

(ii) Surveys   ☐

(iii) Media programming ☐

(iv) Public campaigns   ☐

(v) Other (state):

_____

_____

b)   To what extent are these instruments used? [check box]

to a great extent ☐   somewhat ☐   not at all ☐

Institutional Environment

Women's employment in the media

a)   What is the position of women employed in media organisations?

(i) Name of media organisation:

_____

Medium/media [check box(es)]:

TV ☐ Radio ☐ Video ☐ Film ☐ Newspaper ☐ Ad agency ☐

Percentage of women/men in various areas:

Management:	% males:	% females: ....
Editorial:	% males:	% females: ....
Design:	% males:	% females: ....
Technical:	% males:	% females: ....

(ii) Name of media organisation:

_____

Medium/media [check box(es)]:

TV ☐ Radio ☐ Video ☐ Film ☐ Newspaper ☐ Ad agency ☐

Percentage of women/men in various areas:

Management:	% males:	% females: ....
Editorial:	% males:	% females: ....
Design:	% males:	% females: ....
Technical:	% males:	% females: ....

(iii) Name of media organisation:

_____

Medium/media [check box(es)]:

TV ☐ Radio ☐ Video ☐ Film ☐ Newspaper ☐ Ad agency ☐

Percentage of women/men in various areas:

Management:	% males:	% females: ....
Editorial:	% males:	% females: ....
Design:	% males:	% females: ....
Technical:	% males:	% females: ....

b)   What percentage of women:

(i) stay and progress in the media organisations?

TV ...... % Radio ...... % Video ...... %

Film ...... % Newspaper ...... % Ad agency ...... %

(ii) stay but make little progress?

TV ...... % Radio ...... % Video ...... %

Film ...... % Newspaper ...... % Ad agency ...... %

(iii) drop out before they advance very far?

TV ...... % Radio ...... % Video ...... %

Film ...... % Newspaper ...... % Ad agency ...... %

Codes/guidelines covering sexual harassment at the workplace

a)   Does the organisation have in place codes/guidelines on sexual harassment? [check box]

Yes ☐ No ☐

b)   How clear and effective are these codes/guidelines? [check box]

very clear   ☐   clear   ☐   unclear   ☐

very effective ☐   effective ☐   ineffective ☐

c)   To what extent are the codes/guidelines backed by sanctions? [check box]

to a great extent ☐   somewhat ☐   not at all ☐

d)   Does the policy governing the codes/guidelines include a programme for increasing understanding of what constitutes sexual harassment? [check box]

Yes ☐ No ☐

e) If Yes, to what extent is this programme implemented? [check box]

to a great extent ☐ somewhat ☐ not at all ☐

Flexibility at the workplace

a) Are there policies in place which allow for sympathetic responses to domestic needs? [check box]:

(i) for men? Yes ☐ No ☐

(ii) for women? Yes ☐ No ☐

b) Specify the areas of needs covered by these policies [check box]:

(i) Child-care facilities   Yes ☐ No ☐

(ii) Child-care allowances   Yes ☐ No ☐

(iii) Maternity leave with pay   Yes ☐ No ☐ Without pay? Yes ☐ No ☐

(iv) Paternity leave with pay   Yes ☐ No ☐ Without pay? Yes ☐ No ☐

Training

a) Are training opportunities provided for all staff to examine gender specific issues? [check box]:

(i) as they effect all areas of society and power relationships?

Yes ☐ No ☐

(ii) as they impact the media? Yes ☐ No ☐

b) How clear and effective are these opportunities for all staff to examine gender

(i) as they effect all areas of society and power relationships? [check box]

very clear   ☐   clear   ☐   unclear   ☐

very effective ☐   effective ☐   ineffective ☐

(ii) as they impact the media? [check box]

very clear   ☐   clear   ☐   unclear   ☐

very effective ☐   effective ☐   ineffective ☐

c) Are there programmes in place to [check box]:

(i) help women enter the media/communication industry? Yes ☐ No ☐

(ii) keep women there once they have entered?   Yes ☐ No ☐

(iii) encourage women to continue in-service training?   Yes ☐ No ☐

(iv) give women the knowledge and confidence needed   Yes ☐ No ☐
to tackle gender issues?

d) How clear and effective are these programmes [check box]:

(i) in helping women enter the media/communication industry?

very clear   ☐   clear   ☐   unclear   ☐

very effective ☐   effective ☐   ineffective ☐

(ii) in keeping women there once they have entered?

very clear ☐   clear ☐   unclear ☐

very effective ☐   effective ☐   ineffective ☐

(iii) in encouraging women to continue in-service training?

very clear ☐   clear ☐   unclear ☐

very effective ☐   effective ☐   ineffective ☐

(iv) in giving women the knowledge and confidence needed to tackle gender issues?

very clear ☐   clear ☐   unclear ☐

very effective ☐   effective ☐   ineffective ☐

e)   Are there programmes in place for training in gender sensitive media literacy skills [check box]:

(i) in schools?   Yes ☐ No ☐

(ii) in higher educational institutions?   Yes ☐ No ☐

(iii) at community level?   Yes ☐ No ☐

f)   How clear and effective are these programmes [check box]:

(i) in schools?

very clear ☐   clear ☐   unclear ☐

very effective ☐   effective ☐   ineffective ☐

(ii) in higher educational institutions?

very clear ☐   clear ☐   unclear ☐

very effective ☐   effective ☐   ineffective ☐

(iii) at community level?

very clear ☐   clear ☐   unclear ☐

very effective ☐   effective ☐   ineffective ☐

Data bases

a)   Is there a data base in place about women and media [check box]?   Yes ☐ No ☐

b)   Which of the following areas does the data base cover? [check box(es)]

(i) the place of women in media organisations?   Yes ☐ No ☐

(ii) women in media training organisations?   Yes ☐ No ☐

(iii) women's employment in all areas of the media?   Yes ☐ No ☐

(iv) the level at which women drop out of media organisations?   Yes ☐ No ☐

(v) salary levels among women and men in media organisations?   Yes ☐ No ☐

(vi) the extent to which women are promoted in media organisations?   Yes ☐ No ☐

c)   Are the data stored, maintained and updated regularly? [check box]

Yes ☐ No ☐

d) Are the data used for reviewing policy? [check box] Yes ☐ No ☐

e) If Yes, to what extent are the data used for reviewing policy? [check box]

to a great extent ☐ somewhat ☐ not at all ☐

Technology

a) To what extent are women being encouraged in the use of the new communication technologies? [check box]

to a great extent ☐ somewhat ☐ not at all ☐

b) Which of the following are made available to women? [check box(es)]

i) hardware ☐

ii) software ☐

iii) free training ☐

iv) repackaged 'how-to' information in simple, straightforward, non-sexist, culturally relevant local languages? ☐

Media monitoring

a) Are there internal mechanisms for monitoring media output as it relates to women? [check box] Yes ☐ No ☐

b) Which mechanisms are included? [check box(es)]:

(i) Clippings files Yes ☐ No ☐

(ii) Instruments for analysing visibility of women (e.g., number of women in the news, number of on-air reporters, number of women experts, etc.) Yes ☐ No ☐

(iii) Reports from monitors Yes ☐ No ☐

(iv) Other (specify):

_____

_____

c) Are there media watchdog groups monitoring the state of the media? [check box]

Yes ☐ No ☐

d) To what extent are these media watchdog groups [check box]:

(i) encouraged?

to a great extent ☐ somewhat ☐ not at all ☐

(ii) given status?

to a great extent ☐ somewhat ☐ not at all ☐

Media Environment

The editorial policy

a) Is there an editorial policy in place that ensures that all voices are heard in public media irrespective of race/ethnicity, class/caste, gender, sex? [check box] Yes ☐ No ☐

b) How clear and effective is this aspect of the editorial policy? [check box]

very clear ☐   clear ☐   unclear ☐

very effective ☐   effective ☐   ineffective ☐

c) Does the editorial policy speak to issues related to the portrayal of women? [check box] Yes ☐ No ☐

d) How clear and effective is this aspect of the editorial policy? [check box]

very clear ☐   clear ☐   unclear ☐

very effective ☐   effective ☐   ineffective ☐

e) To what extent were/are women consulted in the formulation of the editorial policy? [check box]

to a great extent ☐   somewhat ☐   not at all ☐

f) Are there mechanisms in place for [check box]:

(i) Monitoring the editorial policy? Yes ☐ No ☐

(ii) Reviewing the editorial policy? Yes ☐ No ☐

g) Are these mechanisms clear and effective? [check box]

very clear ☐   clear ☐   unclear ☐

very effective ☐   effective ☐   ineffective ☐

h) Does the editorial policy include guidelines on the use of gender-sensitive language? [check box] Yes ☐ No ☐

i) How clear and effective are these guidelines? [check box]

very clear ☐   clear ☐   unclear ☐

very effective ☐   effective ☐   ineffective ☐

To what extent does the public media seek the views of women in news and programming [check box]:

a) for expert opinions in media interviews?

to a great extent ☐   somewhat ☐   not at all ☐

b) for views on technical, scientific, medical and other areas traditionally considered to be male domains?

to a great extent ☐   somewhat ☐   not at all ☐

c) as consultants and advisors?

to a great extent ☐ somewhat ☐ not at all ☐

d) as information sources?

to a great extent ☐ somewhat ☐ not at all ☐

Suitability of imported programming

a) To what extent is the content of imported programming examined and considered for its relevance to, and impact on the local community? [check box]

to a great extent ☐ somewhat ☐ not at all ☐

b) Are there local programmes which critically examine the content, relevance and impact of the messages conveyed by imported programmes?

Yes ☐ No ☐

c) To what extent is there co-operation with other countries in the region and/or with similar cultural values in the production of more sensitive programming?

to a great extent ☐ somewhat ☐ not at all ☐

Working with women's media networks

a) To what extent does the ministry support, partner, and/or use the skills/knowledge of women's alternative media networks [check box]?

(i) in joint media productions?

to a great extent ☐ somewhat ☐ not at all ☐

(ii) in public programming (using media productions)?

to a great extent ☐ somewhat ☐ not at all ☐

(iii) in public media programming (hiring women as consultants)?

to a great extent ☐ somewhat ☐ not at all ☐

(iv) in policy-making bodies (appointing women as members)?

to a great extent ☐ somewhat ☐ not at all ☐

(v) in schools and other educational institutions (employing women as trainers)?

to a great extent ☐ somewhat ☐ not at all ☐

(vi) in public media sensitisation programmes (employing women as trainers)?

to a great extent ☐ somewhat ☐ not at all ☐

(vii) other (specify):

_____

_____

Implementation

Is there a person/team in place with responsibility for and authority over the engendering process? [check box]

Yes ☐ No ☐

Does this person/team have a plan? [check box]

Yes ☐ No ☐

How clear and effective is this plan? [check box]

very clear ☐   clear ☐   unclear ☐

very effective ☐   effective ☐   ineffective ☐

Are there adequate resources in place to ensure implementation of the plan? [check box]

Yes ☐ No ☐

To what extent is the plan being implemented? [check box]

to a great extent ☐   somewhat ☐   not at all ☐

Synthesis

Policy environment

a) Most positive aspect(s):

_____

_____

_____

b) Least positive aspect(s):

_____

_____

_____

c) What actions would you propose for improving/upgrading the gender impact on policy?

_____

_____

_____

Institutional environment

    a)   Most positive aspect(s):

_____

_____

_____

    b)   Least positive aspect(s):

_____

_____

_____

    c)   What actions would you propose for improving/upgrading the gender impact on the institutional environment?

_____

_____

_____

Media environment

    a)   Most positive aspect(s):

_____

_____

_____

    b)   Least positive aspect(s):

_____

_____

_____

c) What actions would you propose for improving/upgrading the gender impact on public media?

_____

_____

_____

Implementation

a) Most positive aspect(s)

_____

_____

_____

b) Least positive aspect(s):

_____

_____

_____

c) What actions would you propose for improving/upgrading the implementation of the gender mainstreaming process?

_____

_____

_____

Appendix 2 *Women's media associations and networks*

This listing can be used as a source for information, news, views, updates, facts and figures, and for experts on women/gender and the media.

International

Association for Progressive Communications (APC)
Women's Networking Support Programme, GreenNet Limited/GreenNet Educational Trust, Bradley Close, 74-77 White Lion Street, London, N1 9PF, UK
Tel: (44-171) 713 1941; fax: (44-171) 937 5551
E-mail: apcwomen@laneta.apc.org; URL: http://www.apc.org/women/

International Women's Tribune Centre (IWTC)
777 United Nations Plaza, New York, NY 10017, USA
Tel: (1-212) 687 8633; fax (1-212) 661 2704
E-mail: iwtc@igc.apc.org

World Association of Community Radio Broadcasters (AMARC)
Women's Committee, 3575 Boul. St-Laurent #704, Montreal, Quebec,
Canada H2X 2T7
Tel: (1-514) 982 0353; fax: (1-514) 849 7129

World Association for Christian Communication (WACC)
Women's Desk, 357 Kennington Lane, London SE11 5QY, UK
Tel: (1-171) 582 9139; fax: (1-171) 735-0340
E-mail: wacc@gn.apc.org; URL: http://www.oneworld.org/wacc

Africa

Anglophone West Africa Media Network for Female Journalists (WAMNET)
c/o P.O. Box 2638, Accra, Ghana
Tel: (233-21) 228 282; fax: (233-21) 229 398
Federation of African Media Women-Southern African Development Community (FAMW-SADC)
c/o Zimbabwe Broadcasting Corporation, P.O. Box HG 444, Highlands,
Harare, Zimbabwe
Tel: (263-4) 498 610; fax: (263-4) 498 608

FEMNET
P.O. Box 54562, Nairobi, Kenya
Tel: (254-2) 440 299; fax: (254-2) 443 868

Asia

Asian Network of Women in Communications (ANWIC)
14 Jangpura-B, Mathura Road, New Delhi 110014, India
Tel: (91-11) 619 821; fax: (91-11) 462 3681

Women's Media Network for Asia and the Pacific (WMNAP)
Gender and Development Programme, Asian and Pacific Development Centre,
Pesiaran Duta, P.O. Box 12224, 50770 Kuala Lumpur, Malaysia
Tel: (60-3) 254 8088; fax: (60-3) 255 0316

Canada and the Caribbean

Canadian Women in Communications
372 Bay Street, Suite 1900, Toronto, Ontario M5H 2W0
Tel: (1-416) 363 1880; fax: (1-416) 363 1882

MediaWatch
517 Wellington Street West, #204, Toronto, Ontario M5V 1G1
Tel: (1-416) 408 2065; fax: (1-416) 408 2069

Toronto Women in Film and Television
20 Eglinton Avenue West, Suite 2206, Toronto, Ontario M4R 1K8
Tel: (1-416) 322 3430/322 3648; fax: (1-416) 322 3703

Women's MediaWatch (Jamaica)
P.O. Box 344, Kingston 9, Jamaica W.I.
Tel: (1-876) 926 0882; fax: (1-876) 926 0862
E-mail: wmwjam@toj.com

Europe

European Commission Steering Committee for Equal Opportunities in Broadcasting
Geneesheerstraat 9, 1560 Hoeilaart, Belgium
Tel: (32-2) 657 3726; fax: (32-2) 657 5586

Pandora (European Network of Women in the Audiovisual Arts)
c/o Universite des Femmes, place Quetelet 1A, 1030 Bruxelles, Belgium
Tel: (32-2) 219 6107; fax: (32-2) 219 2943

Appendix 3   *Glossary*

Gender

Gender can be defined as the set of characteristics, roles and behaviour patterns that distinguish women from men which are constructed not biologically but socially and culturally. The sex of an individual is biologically determined, whereas gender characteristics are socially constructed, a product of nurturing, conditioning, and socio-cultural norms and expectations. These characteristics change over time and from one culture to another. Gender also refers to the web of cultural symbols, normative concepts, institutional structures and internalised self-images which, through a process of social construction, define masculine and feminine roles and articulate these roles within power relationships.

Gender analysis

Quantitative gender analysis is the collection and analysis of sex-disaggregated data which reveals the differential impact of development activities on women and men, and the effect gender roles and responsibilities have on development efforts. Qualitative gender analysis is the tracing of historical, political economic, social and cultural forces in order to clarify how and why these differential impacts, roles and responsibilities have come about.

Gender aware/redistributive/transformative policies

Gender-aware/redistibutive/transformative policies seek to transform existing gender relations by changing the distribution of resources and responsibilities to make it more equitable. These policies involve altering the existing balance of power between men and women, addressing not only practical gender needs but strategic gender interests as well.

Gender equality and equity

Although the terms 'equality' and 'equity' are sometimes used interchangeably, they have come to have discrete meanings. 'Equality' refers to sameness or uniformity in the quantity, value and intensity of provisions made and measures implemented for different groups in society, according to gender, race/ethnicity, class/caste, age, disability, and so on, such that these groups have equal opportunity to avail themselves of these provisions. 'Equity' refers to the outcomes of the provisions made and measures implemented, such that they result in all these groups' being able to enjoy the same standard of living, human rights, freedom of conscience, and participation in decision-making on an equal basis.

Gender-inclusive language

This is language which challenges the assumption/tradition that masculine nouns, pronouns and adjectives include both male and female. Examples of gender-inclusive language are 'staff-hours' (rather than 'man-hours'), 'he or she' (rather than 'he'), and 'his or her' rather than 'his'. Gender-exclusive language, by subsuming the female in the male, acts as both a cause and an effect of the invisibility of women's contribution.

Gender mainstreaming

This term may be conceptualised in two different ways: on the one hand it is an integrationist strategy which implies that gender issues are addressed within the existing development policy, strategies and priorities. Hence, throughout a project cycle, gender concerns are integrated where applicable. On the other hand, mainstreaming also means agenda setting, which implies transformation of the existing development agenda using a gendered perspective. These two concepts are not exclusive and actually work best in combination.

Gender-neutral policies

These are policies that are seen as having no significant gender dimension. However, government policies seldom if ever have the same effect on women as they do on men, even if at first sight they may appear to exist in a context where gender is irrelevant. Thus policies which may appear to be 'gender-neutral' are often in fact 'gender-blind', and are biased in favour of males because they presuppose that those involved in and affected by the policy are males, with male needs and interests.

Gender relations

The relative position of women and men in the division of resources and responsibilities, benefits and rights, power and privilege. When used as an analytical category, gender relations shift the focus away from viewing women in isolation from men.

Gender sensitivity

The understanding and consideration of the socio-cultural factors underlying discrimination based on sex, whether against women or men. Gender sensitivity refers to perceptiveness and responsiveness concerning differences in gender roles, responsibilities, challenges and opportunities.

Gender/sex discrimination

The denial of equal treatment, legal rights or fair opportunities to people because of their sex. Gender discrimination may be intentional or systematic. Systematic gender discrimination occurs when the policies and practices of organisations or institutions, and of society itself, prevents opportunities and rights being accorded to persons of a particular sex.

Gender/sex role stereotyping

The over-simplified, traditional and often false representation of a person based on her or his sex. Such stereotypes stem from traditionally accepted gender roles.

Gender-specific policies

These policies take into account gender differentials, and target women or men specifically, but leave the current distribution of resources and responsibilities intact.

Sex

The biological characteristics of males and females.

Sex-disaggregated data

This is data collected – via questionnaires, observation or other techniques – that reveal the different situations, roles and responsibilities of men and women. Having data disaggregated by sex is extremely important to being able to assess the differential impact of a policy or project on women and men.